The
Instructed
Vision

INDIANA UNIVERSITY PRESS

BLOOMINGTON   1961

The
Instructed
Vision

*Scottish Common Sense Philosophy and
the Origins of American Fiction* BY

TERENCE MARTIN

Indiana University Humanities Series Number 48
Indiana University, Bloomington, Indiana

Publication Committee: Edward D. Seeber, Editor; Rudolf B. Gottfried and Hubert C. Heffner, Assistant Editors

The Indiana University Humanities Series was founded in 1939 for the publication of occasional papers and monographs by members of the faculty.

to MY MOTHER
AND FATHER

Foreword

THERE IS a consensus of opinion among scholars that the Scottish philosophy of Common Sense had a crucial function in the establishing of "the American mind." For over fifty years, writes Perry Miller, Scottish realism "constituted what must be called the official metaphysic of America." According to Howard Mumford Jones, it "may be considered the official academic belief" of the first half of the nineteenth century. Similar statements have been made by Merle Curti, William Charvat, Roy Harvey Pearce, and others. The ideas of Thomas Reid, Dugald Stewart, Thomas Brown, Lord Kames, James Beattie, Archibald Alison, and Hugh Blair have come in for study because of their pervasive influence on the American college curriculum in the nineteenth century and, in turn, on those who studied that curriculum. Much specialized study of this influence (on individual colleges, individual men) has been done. Yet, as Leon Howard points out, "the entire matter . . . has by no means been adequately studied."

My purpose in this study is to seek a more adequate understanding of the function of Common Sense thought in the United States by considering its relation to the origins of American fiction. Taught extensively in American colleges and universities, based on metaphysical principles identical with those underlying the prevailing American attitude toward fiction, the philosophy of Common Sense could lend new force to the American suspicion of the imagination at the very time new force was necessary. As we shall see, it offered an enlightened and extremely effective means of controlling the imagination to a society which believed in the need for such control. As a consequence, it contributed to the special problems of the would-be American writer of fiction, for it made fiction more difficult to imagine as an independent, autonomous kind of expression. Yet, as I see it, the implications of Scottish Common Sense thought, suffused into social attitudes, may have pushed the writer who had sufficient audacity toward the creation of the romance, which, by means of its traditional imaginative latitude, could offer him a mode of creative release.

I shall have much occasion in the following pages to use the term *imagination*, which I take to mean that faculty by means of which we explore the order of possibility. Many of the persons with whom this study deals, however, have special theories of the imagination; these I shall elucidate in the course of my discussion. That American suspicion of the imagination has its English counterpart is, of course, obvious; rather than make the point each time I discuss the American attitude toward the imagination, I have postponed comparative comment until Chapter Four. My interest, however, is primarily descriptive and analytical: I seek to establish something of the character of the American imagination.

I wish to thank the Indiana University Graduate School for two grants which enabled me to extend my research. And I am deeply grateful to Roy Harvey Pearce, who suggested such a study to me several years ago and has given generous criticism and relentless help whenever I have called upon his time. My hope is to employ and extend the results of this study in a future consideration of the development of American fiction *per se*. To establish these results satisfactorily, however, to articulate the necessary themes and ideas, I felt that the present study had to come first.

Table of Contents

FOREWORD   vii

Chapter 1—Common Sense Philosophy in America:
    Provenience and Purpose   3
    DEFINITIONS • COLLEGES AND TEXTS •
    AWARENESS AND INFLUENCE • THREE REAC-
    TIONS • IN SUMMARY

Chapter 2—American Fiction and the Metaphysics
    of Actuality   57
    THE CASE AGAINST FICTION • DEFENSIVE
    MEASURES • THE METAPHYSICAL SANCTION •
    CONFIRMATION

Chapter 3—The World Without and the World Within:
    Fiction and the American Imagination   107
    IMAGINATION, REALISM, AND INSTINCT •
    TRANSCENDENCE *vs* THE CULTURE OF THE
    IMAGINATION • IN QUEST OF FICTION •
    THE ROMANCE • THE HAUNTED MIND

Chapter 4—A Note on Society and the Imagination   151

NOTES   167

INDEX   193

Every man of us has a metaphysics, and has to have one; and it will influence his life greatly.

C . S . P E I R C E

A possible object—an *ens rationis*—is a mere fabrication of the mind itself.

S I R W I L L I A M H A M I L T O N

To supplant a reality by a fiction is a preposterous method of diffusing truth.

R E V . D R . J A M E S G R A Y

1

COMMON SENSE PHILOSOPHY IN AMER-
ICA: PROVENIENCE AND PURPOSE

Chapter One

Definitions

IN HIS article on the history of textbooks in logic, ethics, and psychology used in American colleges (1894), G. Stanley Hall explains why the works of the Scottish Common Sense philosophers were so readily adopted as texts by American institutions, especially in the first half of the nineteenth century. In the field of psychology, he says, American professors drew back from the implications of Berkeley and Hume; for the Scottish philosophy represented by such men as Thomas Reid, Dugald Stewart, Thomas Brown, and Sir William Hamilton "opened a far safer way." Its watchword, common sense, "contained an immediate conviction of right and wrong, of the reality of the external world, freedom, etc., about which there was no need or warrant for debate or doubt, while its discussion of association, desire, will, and feeling, was lucidity itself, and fitted our practical country," having a wider vogue here than in Scotland itself. In this form, Hall concludes, psychology and moral philosophy were widely introduced into American colleges, where they had no quarrel with religion, were not unsettling, and were "full of stimulus to the young."[1]

In thus defining the appeal of Scottish Common Sense philosophy to American colleges, Hall anticipates the con-

clusion of later intellectual historians—that the safe, stabilizing, and conservative spirit of Scottish realism was what
made it attractive in early America. I. Woodbridge Riley
points out that it "left little to the imagination, desired no
novel inventions, but preferred to keep its adherents revolv-
ing in the treadmill of traditional thought"; its policy was
"to turn out safe minds content to mark time in the old
way." Merle Curti explains that Scottish philosophy substi-
tuted a common sense assurance of the validity of Christian
morality for the subtleties of the "idealism of Berkeley, the
negations of Hume, and the quasi-materialism of Locke."
It was, he continues, "admirably suited to the needs of
conservative-minded intellectuals" who saw the consolidation of the social order as the prerequisite of successful
commercial and industrial ventures. Roy Harvey Pearce
indicates that by answering to the new-found American
"need for order and growth," Scottish thought made
"rationalism, freedom, and individualism safe, even conservative"; it provided assurance of and a rationale for
progress, and thus became part of an American way of
thinking. And Herbert W. Schneider speaks of the "safe
and sane system of Scottish realism" as an "ideal pattern for
preventing youth from indulging in speculative extremes."[2]

Mr. Schneider also distinguishes, however, between the
earlier and later importance of Scottish thought in America.
Stressing the impact of the Scottish Enlightenment on the
eighteenth-century American Enlightenment, he indicates
that the Scottish appeal to reason and the moral sense first
helped to form an American mentality free from dogmatism,
receptive to new scientific ways of conceiving reality. But
when Common Sense thought became institutionalized in
American colleges, when, largely in the hands of the Presbyterians, it became an apologetic philosophy in the service
of the clergy, it also became, in Mr. Schneider's view, a

"moral sedative" used as an "antidote to the powerful stimulants of the experimental sciences." Thus in the nineteenth
century Scottish philosophy "had ceased to be a critical
stimulant in society and was serving as a purely pedagogical
discipline."[3]

Though it might serve society in turn as "critical stimulant" and as "moral sedative," Common Sense thought
consistently helped to articulate a need for social order in
America. An "academic" philosophy from the time of its
entrance into the Colonies, it suggested stability and bred
a judicious concern for the actual working of society even
before it had become a "purely pedagogical discipline." Not
that all the Scots held precisely the same philosophical positions; they were eminently capable of disagreeing among
themselves. But the disagreements were intramural, as it
were, and it is possible to speak of a Common Sense school
of thought which gained a widely favorable reception in
America. When John Witherspoon introduced the Scottish
philosophy at the College of New Jersey in 1768, wrote
the Reverend Frederick Beasley, "the principles of Reid,
and the Scottish metaphysicians . . . acquired and maintained
undisputed sway," supplanting the "fanciful theories" of
Bishop Berkeley. At that time Beasley, "together with all
those graduates who took any interest in the subject,
embraced without doubt or hesitation the doctrines of the
Scottish school," though later, as Provost of the University
of Pennsylvania, he came to see Common Sense as an over-
simplified form of philosophic inquiry.[4] Samuel Miller, in
his *Brief Retrospect of the Eighteenth Century* (1803),
notes the arrival of Witherspoon "among the events which
contributed to the advancement of literature and science in
our country." He was, Miller says, "the first man who
taught, in America, the substance of those doctrines of the
Human Mind, which Dr. REID afterwards developed with

so much success."[5] Benjamin Rush, who was instrumental in
bringing Witherspoon to America, believed that "his work
will probably preserve his name to end of time."[6] For
twenty-five years President Witherspoon's lectures on moral
philosophy demonstrated to Princeton students the wrong-
ness of other systems and the rightness of Common Sense
philosophy.[7]

Witherspoon's activity in the cause of the American
Revolution provides a link between Common Sense thought
and the rationale for American independence. A member of
the Continental Congress, Witherspoon signed both the
Declaration of Independence and the Articles of Confedera-
tion. But it would be misleading to generalize from this evidence and equate patriotic fervor with an indiscriminate
passion for the new and the free; we need also to remember
the economic and linguistic conservatism that led Witherspoon to oppose paper money and to disapprove of the
Americanization of English. There were areas in which he
would not sanction revolutionary activity. The notable later
careers of many of his students suggest both the degree and
kind of influence that Witherspoon's Common Sense position would have upon the America of his time. Thirteen
became college presidents; one-hundred and fourteen became clergymen, and a number of these served as principals
of academies; six, including James Madison and Henry Lee,
were members of the Continental Congress; twenty were
United States Senators (including Aaron Burr and Richard
Stockton) and twenty-four were members of the United
States House of Representatives; thirteen became governors
of states; three were Judges of the United States Supreme
Court. Other famous graduates included Charles Lee of
Virginia, Attorney-General of the United States; Hugh
Henry Brackenridge, author of *Modern Chivalry* and Judge
of the Supreme Court of Pennsylvania; and Philip Freneau.[8]

Such an enumeration is impressive, suggesting, as it does, that ideas would be disseminated from the top down in the social structure. Trained in law and religion, these are some of the men who would identify with and protect the values of society as they saw them, who would take it upon themselves as a right and a duty to adjudicate social and moral issues. They would speak of literature, politics, society, and man with a common-sense clarity derived in large part from the Scots they had studied.

The role of Scottish realism in the lives of Thomas Jefferson and James Wilson exemplifies the kind of appeal Common Sense thought could and did have in American society. As a youth, Jefferson was enthusiastic about the Scottish philosophers; Adrienne Koch tells us that he had an "extravagantly high" opinion of Kames, whose influence can be seen in Jefferson's discussion of a developing moral sense.[9] In Kames, too, Jefferson found a full exposition of the theory of natural rights, as Gilbert Chinard has indicated in his edition of *The Commonplace Book of Thomas Jefferson*. Articles 557 to 569 of *The Commonplace Book* are taken from Kames's *Historical Law Tracts* (1758). Admitting the undeniable influence of Locke upon Kames's theory, Chinard maintains that Jefferson found most clearly articulated in Kames the combination of ideas which fit his developing conception of democracy. For him Kames was "a master and a guide."[10] Moreover, the work of the Scots, as Roy Harvey Pearce points out, gave Jefferson a way of "bringing into focus and relationship all that he could discover of the Indian" when he was doing his pioneering ethno-historical researches. In Jefferson's thinking we may see the origins of an American idea of savagism, which "takes its form and unity, however amorphous, from the thinking of the Scots whom Jefferson knew well."[11] In this respect, too, Kames was important, for Jefferson had studied his *Princi-*

ples of Morality and Natural Religion (1751), in which
Kames discussed the idea of the moral sense. In 1814 Jefferson praised Kames and quoted the *Principles* from memory,
then, in a statement that suggests his own impression of how
long before Kames had attracted him, explained: "perhaps
I may misquote him, it being fifty years since I read his
book."[12]

Jefferson also knew and respected Dugald Stewart, whom
he called "a great man, and among the most honest living."
Stewart and Destutt de Tracy, he wrote, are the "ablest
metaphysicians living; by which I mean investigators of the
thinking faculty of man."[13] By 1824, when he thanked
Stewart for a copy of *Elements of the Philosophy of the
Human Mind*, Jefferson had long since incorporated the
ideas of other philosophers into the developing pattern of
his thought. He had, for example, found intellectual stimulus in the work of the French ideologues; by means of trans-
lations and commentaries, as Mr. Chinard indicates, he had
introduced the ideas of Destutt de Tracy and the group of
which he was the theoretician into the United States.[14]
Jefferson grew away from Common Sense thought, or
rather, ranged so widely that the Scots lost their original
importance for him. By themselves, he would have found
them too conservative; as a stage in his intellectual development which continued in some respects to sustain the
formulations of a wider experience, he could continue to
respect them. To Stewart he wrote that he had been happy
to see the *Elements* (an "invaluable" study) become "the
text book of most of our colleges and academies, and pass
through several reimpressions in the United States."[15] He
asked also for Stewart's assistance in selecting foreign
teachers for the University of Virginia. For Jefferson, Common Sense thought led finally to the academy, where it
would serve the cause of stability and social order even as

it would allow for democratic liberalism. It had graduated him to other study and to an operative concept of democracy; it might be counted on to train others for similar graduation.

The career of James Wilson affords additional evidence of the influence of Common Sense thought on American public life. Born in Scotland, educated for the clergy at the University of Glasgow when Adam Smith was Rector, a resident at Edinburgh during the time of Adam Ferguson, Wilson came to America in 1765 and studied law with John Dickinson. Benjamin Rush praises him as an eminent lawyer and an enlightened statesman who "rendered great and essential services to his country in every stage of the Revolution"; when he spoke, his mind was "one blaze of light."[16] The author of a widely read pamphlet, *Considerations on the Nature and Extent of the Legislative Authority of the British Parliament* (1774), Wilson was a member of the Continental Congress, a signer of the Declaration of Independence, and a member of the Constitutional Convention in 1787. Yet his opposition to the Pennsylvania constitution of 1776 and his work in drafting that of 1790 helps to characterize him as a leader of the conservatives during "the counter-revolutionary period."[17] After becoming a member of the first Supreme Court of the United States, Wilson offered in 1790 the first course of lectures in law at the College of Philadelphia (now the University of Pennsylvania). As his biographers are fond of pointing out, President and Mrs. Washington, members of Congress, and other dignitaries attended his opening lecture—Philadelphia, of course, being then the nation's capital. These lectures Charles Page Smith terms "a landmark in American jurisprudence." Wilson sought to reconcile "the Anglo-Saxon concept of natural law with the new Common Sense psychology of Thomas Reid, and thus to place the rationalistic spirit of his age, with its hope, its dynamic social aspirations, its enlargement of the intellectual horizon, in the framework of a traditional faith and by so doing to strengthen the structure of orthodoxy and deepen the insights of the infant sociology."[18] He derived his political philosophy from the principles of Common Sense moral philosophy, specifically from the ideas of Thomas Reid, bringing an Anglican and Scholastic tradition to bear on the individual in the terms of Reid's Common Sense. His ultimate emphasis was on man as a responsible member of society, enabled by the moral sense within him to distinguish right from wrong.[19] Wilson's career shows us how it was possible for a man to be both a revolutionary and a conservative; he lent his intelligence to the cause of revolution with no inconsistency to the principles which led him later to seek a valid conservative basis for law and social order in the new United States.

Benjamin Franklin, too, knew Scottish thought and respected its moral implications. He and Lord Kames met in Scotland in 1759 (where Franklin enjoyed six weeks of "the densest happiness" he had ever known) and corresponded from that time on.[20] He praised Kames's *Principles of Equity* (1760) as a book of great value, especially to "colony Judges, as few of them have been bred to the law."[21] Kames's *Introduction to the Art of Thinking* (1761) he termed a "truly valuable" book which sows "thick in the young mind the seeds of goodness concerning moral conduct." Never, Franklin goes on to say, has he seen "more solid and useful matter contained in so small a compass; and yet the method and expression so clear, that the brevity contains no obscurity."[22] Kames gave a copy of *Elements of Criticism* (1762) to Franklin, who, like future generations of Americans, read it with "pleasure and instruction." Here Franklin encountered for the first time the idea that a proper taste in the arts contributes to the improvement of morals; "convinced" of Kames's position, he reported that the work was "universally commended by those who have read it." It contains "much to admire, and nothing to reprove."[23]

The moral framework of Common Sense thought, as Adrienne Koch suggests, constituted hardly more than a "reaffirmation of conventional maxims, attributed as essential furniture of the mind."[24] For Jefferson, James Wilson, and Franklin, as for those that followed them, the work of Reid and Kames and Stewart was valuable because it sowed "the seeds of goodness concerning moral conduct," because it implied concomitantly a kind of moral democracy—a common, and progressive, sense. Each of these men saw from his special point of view a need for order in American society; each found some degree of assurance in Common Sense thought, which, as we see, furnished a least common denominator for a Jefferson and a Wilson, for a "liberal" and a "conservative." Out of the Revolution came a country equipped for political dialectic yet on the whole disposed to assimilate a safe and sane body of thought that would help articulate the generally felt need to stabilize, temporize, and take stock—to "mark time," in I. Woodbridge Riley's words. Discouraging undue speculation, the philosophy of Common Sense would operate as a philosophy of containment. But, as G. Stanley Hall points out, it neither unsettled the mind *nor* closed it against future growth. And so it proved ultimately a temporary measure, something Americans and America lived through, for it anticipated the very transcendentalist-intuitionist ideas it did its best to avoid. Once assimilated, however, this body of thought would contribute much to the prevailing moral and intellectual disposition of society, would, in ways that are difficult but important to trace, furnish it a clearly articulate if latent ideological basis.

The force of conservatism in early American society has long been a subject for comment (and for debate). In 1800 Frederick Gentz contrasted the origin and principles of the American Revolution with those of the French Revolution in a lengthy essay in the Berlin *Historisches Journal*, concluding that the American Revolution was "from beginning to end, on the part of the Americans, merely a *defensive revolution*," while its French counterpart was, "in the highest sense of the word, *an offensive revolution*."[25] The Americans fought to conserve, the French to destroy, institutions and precedents. Alexis de Tocqueville speaks of the gravity and seriousness of Americans and of the fact that in the United States children advance to the responsibilities of adulthood without passing through a period of adolescence. He sees the great advantage of Americans in their having arrived "at a state of democracy without having to endure a democratic revolution."[26] More recently, Clinton Rossiter has spoken of the conservative nature of the American Revolution and of the ideas that went into the Constitution. Conservatism he considers "a major force in politics and culture throughout the first half century of the Republic"; among other things, the conservative in the role of trustee would "identify and protect the real values of the community."[27] (And we shall see that the critic of literature in the early nineteenth century would envision his function in precisely these terms.) In its own right, Scottish realism came to be primarily an instrument of philosophical conservatism, enhanced in its appeal by its capacity to be enlightened and yet safe, admirably fitted for text book use in American colleges, which were, as we know, predominantly sponsored by religious denominations. We shall later consider at some length the manner in which it would lend an intellectual sanction to the conservative predisposition of the American imagination. If we are to appreciate the widespread impact of Common Sense thought, however, we must first attend to the record; to know its history is to bring ourselves to understand its appeal. In an effort to attain a sense of depth and provenience, which, so far as I know, has never been developed in any large detail, I shall draw on the results of a number of special studies of Scottish influence as well as on those of my own investigations.

Colleges and Texts

In 1795 Samuel Stanhope Smith, son-in-law of John Witherspoon, became President of Princeton. He had graduated from the College in 1764, founded the Academy of Hampden-Sydney in 1776, and accepted an appointment as President of Moral Philosophy at Princeton in 1779. Smith championed the cause of Common Sense philosophy, drawing on Witherspoon and the Scots, but his interest in science and his feeling that the proper function of education is to produce responsible citizens stamp him as more representative of native realism.[28] William H. Hudnutt III portrays Smith as an "enlightened conservative," a man caught in the shift to anti-rationalism; his supposed "secularism" drew the fire of such men as Samuel Miller and Ashbel Green, who felt that the College of New Jersey should devote itself more unremittingly to the training of Presbyterian ministers.[29] A member of the American Philosophical Society, Smith gave an address in 1787 "On the Causes of the Variety of Complexion and Figure in the Human Species"; the address was published in the same year with "Strictures on Lord Kaims's Discourse on the Original Diversity of Mankind" added to it.[30] His purpose was to refute Kames's idea that the great physical variance of human beings proved mankind not to be of one species; Smith argued for the unity of mankind, for an original creation, on the grounds of environment and human adaptability. Kames's position, it may be noted, did not represent an official or orthodox Scottish view, as no theory ultimately opposed to the Mosaic account of creation could. More in agreement with the ideas of Reid and Stewart, Smith could disagree with Kames and still deliver his address and write his "Strictures" very much as a Common Sense philosopher. The paper "gave Smith an international reputation as a philosopher and was in many respects his most original and creative accomplishment."[31]

Smith's lectures, like those of Witherspoon, were later collected and published. In 1827 *The American Quarterly Review* praised them highly, saying that Smith's name "stands in the boldest relief" as a moral philosopher.[32] Rejecting the theories of perception of Locke, Berkeley, and Hume, he calls for judgments based on "experience and fact, interpreted by plain common sense."[33] The testimony of the senses must be admitted as true and require no outside, additional evidence. No writer, Smith feels, "has distinguished himself with greater zeal, ability, and success" against the "philosophic delerium" of Berkeley and Hume "than Dr. Reid of Glasgow, first in his treatise on *the human mind*, and afterwards in his essays on the *intellectual*, and the *active powers of man*." Reid is both clear and comprehensive: "to no author is this branch of science, not to Locke himself, more indebted for its approach towards perfection."[34] Smith views the moral sense as a faculty capable of development; since it is empirical (Locke commands this primary kind of respect from Smith), it can be trained in a manner analogous to the other senses. In his lectures he draws explicitly upon the work of Stewart, Kames, Beattie, and Ferguson, in addition to that of Thomas Reid.

Benjamin Rand and Edgeley W. Todd have provided extensive information about the predominant role of Scottish philosophy at Harvard during the first half of the nine-teenth century. Harvard had adopted Blair's *Rhetoric* in 1788, and Joseph Dennie studied from it during his second year there. After studying English grammar, Sidney Willard (Harvard, 1790) moved on to an "abridgement of Blair's Lectures on Rhetoric" and was required to memorize Blair's "definitions and rules."[35] A list of Harvard professors who favored the philosophic and esthetic principles of Scottish realism is imposing, including such names as David Tappan, Levi Hedge, Levi Frisbie, James Walker, and Francis Bowen (especially in the early portion of his career). And the professors of philosophy and pneumatology were not alone in their preference for Scottish thought. According to William Charvat, Edward T. Channing (Boylston Professor of Rhetoric and Oratory from 1819 to 1851) "was perhaps the most important individual of his time in the dissemination of Scotch aesthetic." His lectures, collected and published, reflect "the influence not only of Blair and Kames but of the whole school of Common Sense philosophers. As teacher, as editor of the *North American Review* [1817–1819], and as critic throughout his active career, he was a significant figure in the literary life of the period."[36]

Throughout his thirty-seven years as professor of philosophy at Harvard, Levi Hedge studied and expounded the ideas of Common Sense philosophy. In 1827 he brought out an abridgement of Thomas Brown's *Lectures on the Philosophy of the Human Mind*, by which he hoped to extend the "knowledge and usefulness of this valuable work." In his preface he says that "the lectures of Dr. Brown have been received with much favour by the community, and have found admirers in every class of readers." Brown's "system of the philosophy of the mind has the merit of uncommon simplicity in its elementary principles, and of forcible and various illustration." It is an excellent book "for persons who are forming the intellectual and moral habits."[37] Hedge's edition of Thomas Brown was added to the curriculum sometime between 1827 and 1830 for the course in intellectual philosophy. Interestingly enough, by 1830–31 another course called Moral Philosophy and Natural Theology was using as a text Brown's *Lectures*—the very book Hedge had abridged.[38]

Hedge's *Elements of Logick* had been published in 1816 and was used at Harvard from that time until 1833. It was warmly reviewed in the *North American Review:* its introduction into the curriculum "thereby much improved" the course of studies at Harvard. The reviewer tells us that Hedge's "plan is to collect from the former systems of logick, and from the works of Reid and Stewart, what is suited to his purpose, and mould the materials into a form the most convenient for academical instruction." Hedge has "judiciously and successfully executed" this plan. Any good book, says the reviewer, even on a subject much less important than that of the present work, brings credit to the author; "and this praise is greatly enhanced when the object is the improvement of education, which is to make more broad, and deep, and sure, the foundation that supports the whole superstructure of society."[39] The implications of this final statement are significant for our understanding of Common Sense thought in America. Hedge's *Logick,* grounded in Common Sense principles as much as any logic can be, improves education in what Americans consider to be the right way, in a manner that reinforces the bases of the social order. This is a statement made not from the point of view of the intellectual historian, who can dispassionately judge Common Sense thought to be eminently safe, but from the point of view of someone involved, engaged, and on the spot, someone who speaks out of a felt need for safety, who praises what makes the foundations of his society more sure and gives approbation judicially, as, for the moment, the semiofficial spokesman of his society. The implications of such a statement allow us to see from the inside, as it were. The philosophical conservatism of Hedge as received by the social conservatism of the reviewer are revealed as one, and we are face to face with an authentic valuation of the historical moment.

Deeply influential as a teacher, Levi Frisbie was the first Alford Professor of Natural Religion, Moral Philosophy, and Civil Polity at Harvard (1817–1822). His *Inaugural Address* (1817) indicates his regard for the ideas of Common Sense philosophy. Indeed, Scottish realism, adapted to circumstances as it could be, fit very well the provisions of the John Alford estate for establishing a chair of philosophy: it could encourage religious and civic responsibility by reminding man of his duties as a human being and by showing "the coincidence between the doctrines of revelation and the dictates of reason," never losing sight of "the absolute necessity and vast utility of a divine revelation."[40] Through the teaching of James Walker and Francis Bowen, later Alford Professors, Scottish thought remained influential at Harvard until after the Civil War.[41] Bowen, in 1838, believed Locke to be distinguished for originality rather than for depth, but defended Locke's contribution to philosophy because it led to the common sense inquiry: "and what is philosophy," he asked, "but common sense, employed in abstract investigations?"[42]

All this is not by any means to deny or minimize the importance and influence of "the learned, enlightened, and renowned Locke," as Mercy Warren called him, in American colleges during the same period, which numerous scholars have acknowledged and which Merle Curti has studied in detail.[43] Locke's epistemology, especially, had long held a profound appeal for the American mind. As Todd has pointed out, however, Samuel Gilman had already wondered about the limitations of Locke. In a review of Thomas Brown's *Inquiry into the Relation of Cause and Effect* (1818) in the *North American Review*, Gilman admitted that "Locke is a general classic among our colleges." But in a footnote he asked, "Is not a *System of Metaphysics* wanted for our colleges? Something like a history of opinions in that science, with or without the theories of the compiler. Would Locke obtain more than a respectable chapter in such a system? Brunck, Stewart in his Dissertation, and Degerando would furnish copious and valuable assistance in compiling it."[44] The Harvard catalogue of 1833 announced that in a course where Stewart and Locke were both read the students would be required to criticize Locke by "exhibiting the opinions of other philosophers on controverted questions"; Dugald Stewart would certainly have been of assistance in preparing such criticisms, and perhaps that is one of the reasons why he was included in the course. From his review of courses and textbooks at Harvard, Benjamin Rand concludes that "the introduction of the Scottish philosophy chiefly characterized the progress of philosophical thought at Harvard during the first half of the nineteenth century."[45]

In his study, *The Connecticut Wits*, Leon Howard has shown how the conservatism of Scottish thought won it a place at Yale in the later eighteenth century. Yale students, says Howard, came to college "to acquire the knowledge and literature that would command due deference from the mass and enable them to be entrusted with the power of judging."[46] They found assurance in William Wollaston's *The Religion of Nature Delineated*, which was used by President Thomas Clap in his moral philosophy course. Wollaston was not perfect (Clap criticized his definition of moral virtue in *An Essay on the Nature and Foundation of Moral Virtue*), but his "constant emphasis upon 'matters of fact' and 'things as they are' formed the basis of a practical philosophy so conservative that the ordinary well-bred Connecticut youth must have accepted it as the consummation of all proper ideas."[47] Where Wollaston could thrive Kames could thrive, for their respective moral and esthetic systems complemented each other nicely. Thus, it is no surprise that Kames held an attraction for Yale students. His *Elements of Criticism* "had become so well known in New Haven that it was being advertised in 'a new and cheap edition' by 1770."[48] John Trumbull, Timothy Dwight, and Joel Barlow all studied the *Elements of Criticism* while at Yale.

James Beattie's *Essay on the Nature and Immutability of Truth* (1770) and Hugh Blair's *Rhetoric* were also important at Yale during the late eighteenth century. Yale had adopted the *Rhetoric* in 1785. In 1824 Yale seniors studied Stewart, Blair, and Hedge (together with Locke and Paley).[49] In 1829 Thomas Brown's *Lectures on the Philosophy of the Human Mind* was added to the course in moral philosophy.[50] Like many other American periodicals, the *Christian Spectator*, published at New Haven, praised Scottish philosophy respectfully, even defending as orthodox the ideas of Thomas Brown, the most vigorously criticized member of the Scottish school.

In addition to professors of philosophy and rhetoric, American professors of theology were attracted to Common Sense thought. "The leading thinkers of the American Calvinistic tradition," writes Sydney E. Ahlstrom, "experienced in acute terms the need for an apologetical philosophy" in the late eighteenth and early nineteenth century. Scottish philosophy gave them exactly what they needed.[51] And thus it became part of the course of instruction at divinity schools and theological seminaries. At the Yale Divinity School, Nathaniel William Taylor (from 1822 to 1858) taught a mental and moral philosophy course "steeped in Scottish thought"; both Leonard Woods (1808–1846) and Edwards Amasa Park (1835–1881) at the Andover Seminary advocated the principles of Common Sense philosophy; David Tappan, Hollis Professor of Divinity at Harvard (1792–1803), I have already mentioned as favoring the Scots; and at the Princeton Theological Seminary Archibald Alexander and Charles Hodge supported the Scottish philosophy strongly. Through their efforts, Ahlstrom says, "the Scottish Philosophy was carried by Princeton graduates to academies, colleges, seminaries, and churches all over the country."[52] Moreover, Common Sense thought, eschewing philosophic subtlety whenever possible, could be communicated readily in sermons and tracts. Ahlstrom sees it coming to exist in America "as a vast subterranean influence, a sort of water-table nourishing dogmatics in an age of increasing doubt."[53] This it did and more. Though doubts and energies and needs would eventually diminish its capacity to nourish, the remarkable staying power of Scottish philosophy evidences the strength of the American desire to make sure all was well, all secure, safe, and in working order. Only then would break-throughs come in an imaginative-intuitive quest for a larger, more inclusive kind of reality.

The intricate question of Scottish influence in the West, involving as it does matters of settlement and missionary activity, does not directly concern us here.[54] We know, however, of the persistence of the Scotch Presbyterians in founding schools and perpetuating traditional education. And since Princeton was the training ground for Presbyterian clergy, we can expect that its influence would extend westward. Canonsburg Academy in western Pennsylvania was founded by the Rev. John McMillan of Princeton; when it became Jefferson College, in 1802, the Rev. John Watson of Princeton was its President. The first President of Ohio University, chartered in 1804, was the Rev. Jacob Lindly, also a graduate of Princeton. Robert Hamilton Bishop, whom Louis B. Wright calls "an enlightened Scot," became President of Miami University in 1824. In Indiana the Presbyterians gained control of Vincennes University in 1804 and of the seminary at Bloomington (later Indiana University) in 1820.[55]

Congregationalists from Yale began in the 1820's to rival the Presbyterians as an educational influence in the West. "Most of the trail-blazers were from Princeton," says George P. Schmidt, but both Princeton and Yale deserve the title "mother of colleges."[56] These two schools he terms the most conservative colleges during this period; together they furnished fifty-eight presidents to the seventy-five colleges in operation before 1840. These men succeeded in making Western colleges and academies a good deal like those in the East; men trained in the principles of Scottish Common Sense thought passed along their philosophic bias to the newer Western scholars.[57]

The significance of such influence and passing along can be seen in the reaction of the Rev. John P. Durbin of Augusta College in Kentucky, who, in 1831, urged his Methodist brethren to emulate the educational work of the Presbyterians and Congregationalists. Speaking of the Presbyterians, he enumerates the effects of their emphasis upon education.[58] First of all, they properly educate enough persons "to fill up all the offices, agencies, and employments, presented in the services of the public, or societies," thereby adding "vastly" to their resources and influence. Secondly, "it is a matter of peculiar care with them to have a sufficient number of suitable persons to possess the appointments in

universities, colleges, academies, and common schools, and
to have them introduced into them." Again this gives the
Presbyterians a "vast advantage," for some persons contend
that "the President of a superior college had it in his power
to do more harm or good, than the President of the United
States." Moreover, the plenitude of their educated members
"necessarily gives them persons who seek employment as
editors of political, literary, and religious papers"; consequently, they have a virtual monopoly of the press. Finally,
since the "seminaries generally produce the literati of a
country. . ., the authors, compilers, and editors" of a nation's
books, the Presbyterians have built an "incalculable" advantage in this regard. Their present educational work in the
Mississippi Valley, says Durbin, is astonishing. He urges the
Methodists to learn from the Presbyterians the value of
wedding education in philosophy, literature, and science to
the primary principles of religion.

And the record can be extended. John Blair Smith, a
graduate of Princeton and a Presbyterian minister, succeeded his brother Samuel Stanhope Smith as President of
Hampden Sydney College, then became the first President
of Union College in Schenectady, New York. The famous
President Eliphalet Nott of Union, a Presbyterian minister,
gave a widely ranging course of lectures based on Kames's
Elements of Criticism; in the 1840's, reports Frederick W.
Seward, the course was regarded by students as highly important and was known simply as "Kames."[59] When the
Rev. Charles Nisbet came to America from Scotland in
1785, John Witherspoon thought him a suitable candidate
for the presidency of Princeton; in 1786 he was elected
President of Dickinson College.[60] Asa Mahan of Oberlin
had studied at Andover Theological Seminary and served
as a Presbyterian pastor in Cincinnati before his election as
first President of Oberlin in 1835. Although he was eclectic

in his approach to philosophy, drawing on Cousin, Coleridge, and Kant, and thus not a strict advocate of Scottish realism, the Oberlin curriculum under Mahan included Stewart's *Elements of Intellectual Philosophy*, Kames's *Elements of Criticism*, and, for a while, Francis Wayland's *The Elements of Moral Science*, all books guaranteed to inculcate the Common Sense approach.[61] John Blair Smith, Eliphalet Nott, Charles Nisbet, and Asa Mahan—these are a few of the men who, in different ways, in differing degrees, extended the influence of Scottish thought in the smaller colleges.

The vehicle for the transmission of these (Scottish and other) ideas was the flexible and many-sided moral philosophy course taught in the senior year, often by the college president. In *The Old Time College President*, George P. Schmidt presents an admirable account of this course.[62] He finds it to be basically didactic, intended "to prepare students for intelligent service in the community and nation."[63] As an instrument for molding proper public attitudes, the course at one time included political, sociological, and economic material, all subsumed under the dominant moral principle. Ultimately these sub-subjects developed into independent courses of study.[64] But for several decades the college president could use the moral philosophy course as his personal sounding board; understanding this, we may understand why men who had taken the course would bring "sectarian judgments and theological compulsions to bear upon their decisions" in public life.[65] Schmidt finds a basic unity amid personal and philosophic diversity in the course and concludes that it materially influenced "the thought and action of the leaders of the age," constituting as it did the final and climactic aspect of formal education.[66] This view is supported by the fact that in 1829, in addition to the colleges discussed earlier, such colleges as Dartmouth, Middlebury, Amherst, Williams, Washington, Union, Hamilton, Geneva, Jefferson, and Transylvania used Stewart or Kames or, more frequently, both in the senior year.[67]

William Charvat has indicated the pervasive influence of Kames's *Elements of Criticism* and Blair's *Rhetoric* in the first part of the nineteenth century. At least thirty-one editions of *Elements of Criticism* appeared, nine before 1835. Fifty-three editions of Blair's *Rhetoric* were published in America, thirty-nine of them before 1835. It became a standard text for courses in rhetoric, and, between 1800 and 1835, was adopted by Columbia, Pennsylvania, Brown, North Carolina, Middlebury, Williams, Amherst, Hamilton, Wesleyan, and Union.[68] Investigating the effect that Blair and Kames had on the concept of nationality in America, Benjamin Spencer sees them as the most influential critical authorities of the postrevolutionary generation. The *Boston Magazine* cited Blair as early as 1783; from that time on such writers as Joseph Ladd, John Blair Linn, and Charles Brockden Brown used Blair and his promptings of the heart to combat the denationalizing effects of neoclassical principles.[69] Kames, as we know, urged attention to grand and elevating objects, finding them to be universally agreeable and, by extension, supranational. But the fact that sublime subjects could be found so specifically and concretely in America caused Americans to investigate the local with increasing intensity as a means of achieving a universal standard of taste. Kames allowed Americans to be universal by being particular; once having been particular, some Americans had to readjust and re-emphasize Kamesian principles; in the meantime, however, *Elements of Criticism* continued to be republished.

But even a complete listing of all books of the Scottish school used in the United States would not tell the whole story of the influence of their thought upon American education. For the American editions and versions of Brown, Stewart, and especially of Blair and Kames expanded the Scottish influence tremendously. For example, an edition of *Elements of Criticism* edited by the Rev. James R. Boyd was published in New York in 1868. In his Preface, Mr. Boyd says "we are all greatly indebted" to Lord Kames for his valuable study "and for preparing a work that has long occupied a place in the colleges and academies of our own land." But, although there is no other work that can take its place, and although it cannot be laid aside "without great disadvantage to the cause of education," it can certainly be improved, he believes, with the proper amendments and additions from other writers.[70] Mr. Boyd then sets out to improve Kames, and in a section on the emotions and passions in which he thinks Kames gives only a partial view of the danger of fiction he buttresses the argument by appealing to "Dr. Beattie in his Moral Science."[71] The deficiencies of one Scot are made up for by the excellences of another.

Abridgments were plentiful, and so were American books on mental and moral philosophy which owed conceptual allegiance to the Scots.[72] In the Reverend Asa Burton's *Essays on Some of the First Principles of Metaphysicks, Ethicks, and Theology* (1824) one can see the influence of Reid and Stewart. Thomas C. Upham, Professor of Moral and Mental Philosophy at Bowdoin College, brought out his *Elements of Intellectual Philosophy* in 1827; in 1831 he expanded it into the two-volume *Elements of Mental Philosophy*. The work reveals a thorough knowledge of the Scots; Upham's ideas are fundamentally those of Reid and Stewart, although the plan of his *Mental Philosophy* is to present different points of view and he demonstrates great respect for Locke. Out of Francis Wayland's lectures on ethics and moral philosophy at Brown University came his *Elements of Moral Science* (1835), "the textbook in ethics that had the widest acceptance by America in the second generation of the 19th century."[73] Designed as a text, his book aimed to be "simple, clear, and purely didactic." Wayland speaks primarily from his own common sense, but the basis of his philosophical exposition is in accord with the ideas of Reid and Stewart.

We may illustrate the manner in which the Scots influenced American writers on mental and moral philosophy by considering briefly a typical treatise, Ezra Stiles Ely's *Conversations on the Science of the Human Mind* (1819). The Rev. Dr. Ely, a Presbyterian pastor in Philadelphia, selects what he "deems true and most important" from a number of "celebrated authors," among them Locke, Hume, Kames, Reid, Stewart, and Beattie. He hopes that his *Conversations* will "prove beneficial to Students in Law, Medicine, and Divinity; and to the most intelligent young ladies of our country." He "disdains all *metaphysics* but those of *common sense*."[74] In his conversations with the "Professor," the "Pupil" admits he had "thought all metaphysical reasonings unintelligible and useless; especially if they related to the human soul." Until he studied the works of Reid and Stewart at the Professor's suggestion, he "was ready to despair of obtaining any distinct and satisfactory conception on this subject."[75] The Pupil calls for a systematic exposition of the science of the human mind without the "metaphysical jargon and nonsense" which have "disgusted many, and induced the great body of people to believe, that one who would become a metaphysician must renounce common sense." Unfortunately such a treatise does not exist, says the Professor, though it is greatly to be desired (and is, in fact, what Ely is attempting to write). "Dr. Reid," he continues, "who has excelled all other writers on this subject, employed himself rather in demolishing an old fabrick, than in building up a new one." Stewart he sees as "but an elegant commentator upon Reid, without originality, and without any comprehensive arrangement of the topics of mental science."[76] Proceeding then to his systematic exposition, Ely draws heavily on the Scots, especially Thomas Reid, whose ideas and definitions constitute the guiding genius of the book. Ely's *Conversations* is typical not because of his personal preference among the Scots (indeed, he enters a minority opinion on Stewart), but because of his insistence that no approach to the subject of mental science surpasses the common sense approach and his explicit dependence on the ideas of the Scottish school.

Awareness and Influence

In 1803 Samuel Miller published his *Brief Retrospect of the Eighteenth Century*, the first attempt at systematic intellectual history in the new Republic. Throughout his two volumes, Miller surveys the advance of knowledge in the preceding century, compiling and judging the results of work in such areas as mechanical philosophy, medicine, geography, mathematics, agriculture, physiognomy, philosophy of the human mind, and literature. A Presbyterian clergyman trained at Princeton in the principles of Common Sense thought, Miller would, of course, think highly of the Scots. In his *Brief Retrospect*, however, he adopts the role of discriminating historian and shows us the manner in which he would, as it were, meet the public at large, conscious of the "numerous and great" limitations of his study, but hopeful that what he has done will be of value to the public.

Miller characterizes the Common Sense movement as a revolt from "the sceptical conclusions which BERKELEY and HUME had drawn from the old theory of perception, as it had been taught, in substance, by all writers, from

PYTHAGORAS down to" the middle of the eighteenth century. Berkeley and Hume, he contends, were end-products; if they were correct, philosophy had come to a logical conclusion, leaving one without causality, without an extramental world around him. But for Thomas Reid, the first of the Common Sense school, there was one last appeal to be made, a final method of escaping a universal ideality. Miller nicely epitomizes the essential nature of Reid's position:

he totally rejected the ideal system, or theory of perception, as taught by his predecessors, and maintained, that the mind perceives not merely the ideas or images of external objects, but the external objects themselves; that when these are presented to our senses, they produce certain impressions; that these impressions are followed by correspondent sensations; and these sensations by a perception of the existence and qualities of the objects about which the mind is employed. He contended that all the steps of this process are equally incomprehensible; that we can assign no other reason for these facts taking place, but that such is the constitution of our nature; and that when sensible objects are presented to us, we become persuaded that they exist, and that they possess the qualities which we witness, not by a train of reasoning, by formal reflection, or by association of ideas; but by a direct and necessary connection between the presence of such objects and our consequent perceptions. In short, the great and distinguishing peculiarity of this class of metaphysicians is, that they appeal from the delusive principles and shocking conclusions of their opponents, to the *common sense* of mankind, as a tribunal paramount to all the subtleties of philosophy.

Aware of what Thomas Reid and other Scottish philosophers have done, Miller is grateful for deliverance from "delusive principles" and "shocking conclusions," thankful to be in a world where his senses are in indisputable contact with reality. He considers the work of the Scots to be "among the most memorable of the age," perhaps "the most important accession which the philosophy of mind has received since the time of Mr. Locke."[77]

Hocquet Caritat, proprietor of a famous New York City circulating library, pays deference to Dugald Stewart in the *Explanatory Catalogue of H. Caritat's Circulating Library* (1804). In an introductory essay, "On the Use of Books," he refers to Stewart as a writer "to whose merit no praises can do justice" and quotes with approval Stewart's statement that one's reading must be done selectively and with reflection if it is not to weaken the intellectual, inventive, and moral powers.[78] Further praise of Stewart comes from the *Monthly Anthology and Boston Review* of July, 1808. In a "Sketch of the Literary Institutions of Edinburgh" the writer says that

among the classes of general literature in this university, none has acquired such high and deserved celebrity as that of moral philosophy, conducted by professor Stewart. An anonymous tribute of applause could add little to the reputation which this gentleman has obtained as an acute inquirer into moral and metaphysical truths; as an eloquent and animated teacher of philosophy; as the accomplished and feeling biographer of departed merit. In no respect, certainly, are the talents of Mr. Stewart more eminently conspicuous, than in the discharge of his publick duties as a professor. The subject entrusted to his care is one of peculiar importance and difficulty; interesting to every individual of mankind, it involves questions of so complex and intricate a nature, that its verbal elucidation can only be expected from a combination of the most rare and imposing talents. Mr. Stewart's excellence as a lecturer on moral philosophy is principally derived from three circumstances: the accuracy and proportion displayed in his arrangement of subjects; the facility with which he invests his ideas in all the elegancies of language; and the extreme copiousness and beauty of the illustrations, which he always lends to the immediate object of discussion. In these points, perhaps, his merits are unequalled.

But such generous praise of Stewart is not a blanket approval of the Common Sense school of philosophers. The only possible flaw in Stewart's "philosophical character," continues the writer, "is a too rigid adherence to the metaphysical opinions of Dr. Reid, who, though he was undoubtedly an ingenious man, and the founder of a distinct school of philosophy, cannot certainly be ranked among the metaphysicians of the first class." Reid's "frequent misapprehension" of Berkeley, Hume, and others hangs "as a dead weight upon his reputation." Stewart, however, "publickly opposes the ancient theory of ideas, as well as the modernized doctrine of materialism and philosophical necessity; while he admits the principle of common sense as a valid and competent authority in inquiries of this nature."[79]

James Marsh and Thomas Cooper, neither of whom advocated Common Sense philosophy, provide further testimony of American awareness of Scottish realism and its special kind of influence. Marsh, President of the University of Vermont, seems to have recognized that the Coleridgean idealism he espoused would find as its greatest obstacle in the United States the philosophy of Common Sense; in 1829 he brought out an edition of Coleridge's *Aids to Reflection*, with a "Preliminary Essay" in which he pointed out the limitations of Locke and the Scottish school of philosophers.[80] The same year, however, in a letter to Coleridge, he wrote: "The works of Locke were formerly much read and used as text books, in our colleges; but of late have very generally given place to the Scotch writers; and Stewart,

Campbell and Brown are now almost universally read as the standard authors on the subjects of which they treat."[81] In speaking out vigorously against the Scots, the militantly materialistic Thomas Cooper defines in precise though pejorative terms part of the appeal Scottish realism possessed for Americans. "Messrs. Reid, Oswald, Beattie, Dugald Stewart, and Thomas Brown have had their day," says Cooper: "They are favorites with the clergy, for they are of the orthodox school of ideology; they are ontologists and psychologists; they offend no popular prejudices; they run counter to no clerical doctrines; they express due horror at the tendencies of heterodox metaphysics; their style of writing is for the most part good, frequently marked by elegance and taste; while the dogmatism that pervades their pages of inanity is well calculated to impose upon the numerous class of readers who are content to read without thinking." Cooper, who thought that a true metaphysics must be based on physiological principles, believes that "the progress of accurate physiology has destroyed" the Scots, that "the thinking part of the public which ultimately gives the tone to the much larger part that does not think, is wearied with toiling through pages after pages of figurative words and phrases without distinct meaning, and calls aloud for facts in the matter, and precision in the language."[82] Apparently Cooper, who ran cross-grain to society most of his life, did not realize or did not accept the fact that a large part of the educated American public—"the thinking part of the public"—believed the Scots to have a monopoly on "facts," on "distinct meaning," on "precision in the language." The substance of his criticism is to be expected (though the tone is all his own): no proponent of materialism could favor the Common Sense philosophy, which was so well entrenched that to oppose it meant to oppose much that gave shape to the social order—orthodox religion, the general moral disposition of society, the assurance engendered by conservatism.

That not all the copies of Scottish books existed for formal classroom use or in university libraries is shown by the holdings of the Farmer's Library. Founded in 1805 in Wheatland, New York, the Farmer's Library was one of the most important and durable of the numerous subscription libraries, continuing in existence until after the Civil War. Between 1805 and 1825 the library acquired an abridgment of Blair's *Lectures on Rhetoric*, the two volumes of Blair's *Sermons*, James Beattie's *Elements of Moral Science*, Stewart's *Philosophical Essays*, Locke's *Essay Concerning Human Understanding*, and William Paley's *Natural Theology* and *The Principles of Moral and Political Philosophy*. Later acquisitions included a complete two-volume edition of Blair's *Lectures on Rhetoric and Belles Lettres*, Kames's *Elements of Criticism*, and Francis Wayland's *The Elements of Moral Science*. The Library also held a subscription to the *Edinburgh Review*.[83]

As one might expect, many American men of letters came under the influence of Scottish thought at some point in their careers. Archibald Alison's *Essay on the Nature and Principles of Taste* (1790), for example, was important in the formation of William Cullen Bryant's early esthetic concepts, as W. P. Hudson has shown. Through Alison, Bryant became acquainted with the principles and critical methods of the Scottish school of esthetics; his "Lectures on Poetry" (1826) reflect his study of Alison's theory of association.[84]

In demonstrating the source of Emerson's conception of the "moral sense" or "reason," Merrell Davis indicates Emerson's indebtedness to the ideas of Dugald Stewart and the Scottish school. As a sophomore at Harvard, Emerson used Blair's *Rhetoric;* he studied logic from Levi Hedge's *Elements of Logick;* with Levi Frisbie, whom he praised in his journal, he studied Stewart's *Elements of the Philosophy of the Human Mind,* reading Stewart's *Outlines of Moral Philosophy* outside the curriculum.[85] His Bowdoin Prize essay, "A Dissertation on the Present State of Ethical Philosophy," written in 1821, reveals a familiarity with Scottish Common Sense thought. Emerson believed that Thomas Reid's opposition to the "pernicious ingenuity" of Hume and Berkeley by means of "common-sense philosophy" had not completely removed the "terror which attached to the name of Hume."[86] Yet "the first true advance" in moral science belongs to "the school in which Reid and Stewart have labored."[87] When he taught in his brother William's school in the early 1820's, most of Emerson's philosophical instruction came from Thomas Reid, Dugald Stewart, and Thomas Brown.[88] Miss Hannah Stevenson, one of his students, later told Edward Emerson that "to praise Dugald Stewart's Philosophy, which he had lately read, and which was one of the few metaphysical works he liked, was a way to please him."[89] "Stewart's last Dissertation," Emerson wrote in 1822, "saves you the toil of turning over a hundred tomes in which the philosophy of Mind, since the Revival of Letters, is locked up."[90]

Thoreau also came under the influence of Scottish thought at Harvard (1833–1837), though, like Emerson, his later preference was for other avenues to truth and reality. He studied rhetoric with Edward T. Channing and philosophy with Joel Giles and Francis Bowen, all of whom strongly favored Common Sense philosophy at that time.[91] James Kwiat finds that Thoreau's essay "Provincial Americans" (1837) evidences the influence both of Stewart's *Elements of the Philosophy of the Human Mind* and, indirectly, of Reid, "even to the extent of a marked verbal dependence."[92] By 1838, however, Thoreau felt that the intuitive approach had greater potentiality for one whose ultimate mission would be self-exploration. He was "rapidly breaking away" from Scottish realism—beginning the transition that was to make transcendentalism possible for him.[93]

Stewart's *Elements* likewise influenced the thinking of James Russell Lowell. As a senior at Harvard, Lowell studied moral philosophy, without much academic success, under James Bowen; and although he never mentioned Stewart specifically in later years, Lowell "seems to have placed more confidence" in ideas derived from Stewart than in those of other writers.[94] Leon Howard suggests that Lowell may have turned to Stewart's *Elements* in preparing for the Lowell Institute lectures which he gave during January and February of 1855. "The pattern of Stewart's aesthetic thought, rather than the specific expression of his ideas," dominated Lowell's approach to literature in these lectures.[95] Patterns, casts of mind, at times stylistic echoes or explicit formulations: such are the ways in which we trace the effects of early formal study of Common Sense thought in the later careers of men of letters, clergymen, lawyers, educators, and other public men.

But one did not need to go to college to encounter Scottish philosophy. Largely self-educated, throughout his life an omnivorous reader, Orestes Brownson states that he had first gone to school to Locke, "like most English and Americans of my generation." He had then "passed to the Scottish school of Reid and Stewart, and had adhered to it without well knowing what it was, till it was overthrown by Dr. Thomas Brown, who . . . revived the scepticism of Hume, and drove me into speculative atheism, by resolving cause and effect into invariable antecedence and consequence, thus excluding all idea of creative power or productive force."[96] That Thomas Brown drove Brownson into "speculative atheism" does not mean, of course, that he had the same effect on all readers; Brownson, as we know, had a way of being unique. Yet Brown's ideas certainly stirred up more controversy in the United States than did those of any other Scottish philosopher. Much more a secular thinker (a Doctor of Medicine, not of Divinity) than Reid, Stewart, Kames, or Beattie, Brown was at times regarded as a threat to social and religious orthodoxy because of his rationalistic approach to philosophical matters. (He believed, for example, that Hume's views on causality were erroneous but not dangerous.) We have noted, however, that his work was used at Andover and was defended at Yale. Opponents of Brown felt that his *Inquiry into the Relation of Cause and Effect* (1818), controverting Reid on the matter of causality as it did, dragged the old bogey of Hume into the open again, thereby encouraging scepticism and religious doubt. Brownson read Brown correctly: he did hold that cause and effect were terms for "invariable antecedence and consequence." But for Brown there were also "casual" antecedence and consequence. An eclipse of the sun followed by a plague is not a causal or "power" phenomenon; the eclipse, casually antecedent, has no power to cause the plague; for power, as we comprehend and explain our universe, consists of invariability. When one action invariably follows another (invariable antecedence and consequence), we describe the relation of the two actions as one of power, or cause and effect. We learn of power through invariability, or casualness through variability. Thus, Brown does not deny that *A* has the power to cause *B;* he sets up criteria, however, for deciding whether such is (invariably) the case.[97] Proponents of Brown felt that he had made courageous philosophical investigations which did no intellectual violence to God's world or to the orthodoxy which sustained it. And Brown himself thought his idea of causality entirely consistent with a belief in God and in the possibility of miracles.

Though not an advocate of Scottish realism, Brownson believed that any valid philosophical investigation must be based on the principles of common sense. He defines common sense as the simple, universal, "spontaneous beliefs of Humanity"; the "precise object" of philosophy is to explain and verify these beliefs. "We by no means reject common sense," he asserts; "we love, we obey it, because we have legitimated its right to be loved and obeyed. All true philosophy accepts, and explains, and legitimates, the instinctive beliefs of mankind. Philosophy, therefore, though it is not common sense, is in perfect harmony with it." Anticipating the judgment of later commentators, he concludes that common sense "satisfies curiosity, and prevents inquiry from becoming doubt."[98] Brownson's awareness of the Scots is reflected throughout his writing. In a review of Samuel S. Schmucker's *Psychology; or Elements of a New System of Mental Philosophy on the Basis of Consciousness and Common Sense* (1842), he finds the inquiry naive and out of date, "rarely up with the Scottish school of Reid and Stewart." Even Thomas Upham's *Elements of Mental Philosophy* (1839), unquestionably "meagre," he finds superior to Schmucker.[99] Critical of Thomas Reid, Brownson nonetheless calls him "one of the great men of the eighteenth century."[100] But his most unreserved praise goes to Sir William Hamilton, "decidedly the most learned man of the Scottish school," a man of "rare sagacity, and after old Ralph Cudworth, perhaps, the most really erudite philosophical writer in our language"; Hamilton has what Reid lacked— an "acuteness and knowledge of systems."[101] Brownson's comments, copious and intelligent, illustrate further the extent to which Americans were aware of Common Sense thought—its importance, its function, its place in history.

Indispensable to anyone who would know about the Scottish influence on literary criticism is William Charvat's *The Origins of American Critical Thought, 1810–1835,* the pioneer study of periodical criticism in America. Mr. Charvat has found that this criticism "was the work of a practically homogeneous upper class which felt itself competent to legislate, culturally, for other classes. Indeed it took that task upon itself as a duty and often said so specifically." This body of criticism Mr. Charvat terms "judicial"; appearing for the most part anonymously, it drew its authority from established principles assumed by the upper and educated class rather than from individual opinion.[102] Thomas Reid, for example, believed that the word *sense* always implied judgment in its popular usage. "A man of sense is a man of judgement," explains Reid. "Good sense is good judgement. Nonsense is what is evidently contrary to right judgement." Common sense therefore becomes "that degree of judgement which is common to men with whom we can converse and transact business."[103] Significantly enough, then, the American critics were predominantly clergymen and lawyers, men trained, that is, to judge the *common* (public) sense, to adjudicate in terms of established principles; together they could safeguard and transact the business of the social order, one group watching religious, the other secular interests, which could not, of course, finally be separated. "Our criticks and reviewers," said Levi Frisbie with approbation in his *Inaugural Address* at Harvard, "are exercising jurisdiction not only upon the literary but moral blemishes of the authors, that come before them."[104]

Many of the critics studied by Mr. Charvat show in some degree that they have gone to school to the Scottish philosophers and estheticians. Before 1830, for example, the criticism of W. H. Prescott showed both a stylistic and conceptual indebtedness to Scottish thought.[105] Praising

Dugald Stewart in his *American Review of History and Politics*, Robert Walsh wrote that he had intended to review Stewart's philosophical essays in detail, but that he had been anticipated by the *Edinburgh Review*.[106] Charvat terms Walsh's two-volume collection of essays, *Didactics: Social, Literary, and Political* (1836), "a monument to the influence of Scotch philosophy and aesthetics on the American mind."[107] In one of these essays (dated 1825), Walsh congratulates the Pennsylvania Academy of Fine Arts on their good fortune in acquiring a portrait of Dugald Stewart painted by Sir Henry Raeburn, a copy of which was to be given to the Academy of Fine Arts in South Carolina. "No living writer is held in higher estimation in America than Dugald Stewart," says Walsh: "Most of the Americans who have cultivated letters, have read some or all of his works; not a few of us have heard him teaching from his Chair the most exalted philosophy in the noblest strains of eloquence."[108]

Harvard-educated Samuel Gilman helped to make the ideas of Thomas Brown better known in America with three essays in the *North American Review;* he preferred Brown to Reid and Stewart on the grounds that Brown was a more original thinker. In the first of these articles, actually a review of Brown's *Inquiry into the Relation of Cause and Effect*, Gilman admits that "the philosophy of the late lamented Dr. Brown is scarcely known in this country. It was presumed," he continues, "that considerable interest would attach among us to the speculations of the successor of Dugald Stewart, whose own work on the Mind has passed, we believe, through as many editions in the United States as in Great Britain, and who is well known on becoming emeritus, to have warmly recommended Dr. Brown to the chair of moral philosophy in the university of Edinburgh." There is, however, a "vague belief" among those only partially acquainted with Brown's work that his ideas are too close to those of Hume. Gilman's self-imposed task is to analyze Brown's concepts faithfully "and redeem Dr. Brown's reputation."[109] In 1830, in the *Christian Examiner*, Gilman defended the relevance of the teachings of Blair and Alison to a stable and Christian life, crediting Blair with having "brought religion into the parlour."[110]

Moreover, as Robert E. Streeter has ably shown, association psychology—principally as expounded in Archibald Alison's *Essays on the Nature and Principles of Taste* (1790)—fostered the cause of literary nationalism in the *North American Review*. Caught up in what Martin Kallich has called "the associationist climate of opinion," in a tradition deriving from Hobbes and Locke and including such men as Hutcheson, Hume, and Addison, critics of the Scottish school could explain modes of esthetic response by reference to well-known principles of association; largely through their work association psychology became the most "immediately serviceable" body of aesthetic thought "in the advocacy of nationalism."[111] Critics who based their campaign for a national literature on associationist principles were William Tudor, John Knapp, G. C. Verplanck, Samuel Gilman, W. H. Gardiner, and William Cullen Bryant. A minority of critics—among them Walter Channing, E. T. Channing, Jared Sparks, and George Bancroft—used the same generally known principles to combat the nationalist tendency. The list is impressive; the critics who employed associationist psychology were among the best known of the day.

Three Reactions

I should like to complete this survey of the provenience and purpose of Common Sense thought in late eighteenth and early nineteenth century America by examining in some detail three contemporary articles. In an evaluation of ideas, the evidence supplied by quantity must always leave us a little short of our goal if, as historians, we ask ourselves why any given idea has prevailed over other ideas. For the answer to this question is suffused as life and belief under the forms of past experience and yields itself up, if at all, only to attempts to grasp the quality of that experience: to know the function and meaning of an idea as it existed in history is to begin to know the quality it possessed. Though we may never know it fully, our commitment is to discover what we can.

Despite the predominant note of approbation in American comment on Scottish Common Sense thought, I have selected two adverse opinions and one which favors it thoroughly and explicitly. The hostile criticisms mark out for us, as it were, the boundaries of Common Sense influence; they are in the nature of minority reports, acknowledging, even as they argue against, the dominance of Common Sense thought. By seeing how this body of thought could be challenged, moreover, we come to see also the latent grounds for debate. I shall consider Alexander H. Everett's essay, "History of Intellectual Philosophy" (1829), Charles Astor Bristed's "Scotch School of Philosophy and Criticism" (1845), and, turning back chronologically, a review-article dealing with Levi Frisbie's *Inaugural Address* (1818).

Alexander H. Everett had recently returned to America from intermittent diplomatic missions that occupied almost two decades when he wrote his "History of Intellectual Philosophy" for the *North American Review* in 1829. A graduate of Harvard (1806) and a former student of Scottish thought, he had become thoroughly acquainted with French and German literature, had flirted with Kantianism, and finally put his philosophic faith in Locke. In his article he testifies to the importance of Locke in the United States.

Everett's strictures on Scottish philosophy reveal a double philosophical commitment—to the Scots and to Locke: he believed that the reality of the material world was "susceptible of a very easy, and at the same time perfectly rigorous demonstration." As a consequence, he thought that Thomas Reid had over-reacted, that the refutation of idealism is not so difficult as Reid had made it seem. Apparently not realizing that existence "is implied in the facts of perception, and of course proved by them," Reid posited an "instinctive and irresistible belief," a "*common sense*." For Everett this is an unnecessary step; "common sense and philosophy," he says, "are different modes of stating the same facts."[112] He continues: "If then the writers of the Scotch school mean to represent their elementary principles as mere expressions of the common opinion of the world, and as being in that character the incontestable foundations for all our knowledge, it is evident that their propositions have not even the form of a philosophical system." The alternative interpretation is that "they mean to represent the common opinion of the world in favor of their elementary principles, as a kind of *instinctive conviction*, which forms, as it were, a part of the original substance of the mind of every individual"; this alternative, however, Everett sees as leading to a theory of innate ideas, which he feels the Scottish philosophers have not "developed and proved as such."[113]

As an attempt to "reform the theory of Locke respecting the origin of knowledge," Scottish philosophy seems, therefore, of "little value." Nonetheless, Everett concedes that it has been of great importance. He thinks highly of Stewart's analyses of the intellectual powers, but does not like Thomas Brown, "whose 'Lectures' have attracted a good deal of attention in this country."[114] "We consider his 'Lectures,'" Everett writes, "as belonging, in the main, to a class of books more dangerous and mischievous than any other, those in which false and vicious principles are maintained with honest conviction by persons of undoubted good intentions, and clothed in such a dress as not to shock the moral feelings of the public. Presented in this questionable shape, these principles are unsuspectingly adopted by minds that would not otherwise have come in contact with them"; their necessary effects are "in no way neutralized by the skin-deep gilding under which the poison was exhibited." Brown's style, according to Everett, "might be called good" in a promising schoolboy. It is "easy and copious, but verbose, feeble, and overlaid with tasteless ornament and trivial learning," forming a "sorry contrast with the manly and significant simplicity of the 'Essay on the Human Understanding.'" He regrets "that the work has obtained so much currency among us" and hopes "that it will not long be allowed to usurp, in our most respectable institutions for education, the place which was once occupied by the great master of intellectual science."[115]

The tone of Everett's essay is clearly judicial; he is concerned about society and education and the possible warping of minds by the ideas of Thomas Brown. With his contemporaries he shares a commitment to safeguard society, to test and judge ideas for their social validity, for what ultimately amounts to social orthodoxy. Everett's dissent—and it does seem a dissent—is made only in the name of society. His initial criticism of Scottish thought, however, his contention that Thomas Reid went to too much trouble in refuting Berkeley and Hume, is indeed curious. Throughout most of his essay Everett seem to be out-commonsensing the Common Sense philosophers. Needlessly postulating an extra faculty, they have run into the problem of innatism, he believes; they have invented unnecessary machinery and caught themselves up in it. Everett's criticism implies a more economical use of common sense; and it is by means of his streamlined, uncluttered approach, not by means of anything he learned from Locke, that he launches his attack. Ultimately, of course, he advocates Locke, but only after implying a super-realism whereby the reality of the material world proves itself to be in self-evident existence. Anomalous as it may be, Everett appears to agree with the Scots on a theory of being and with Locke on a theory of knowledge.

In 1845 *The American Review* carried a criticism of Scottish philosophy from a different point of view—Charles Astor Bristed's "Scotch School of Philosophy and Criticism." Bristed, grandson of John Jacob Astor, had graduated from Yale in 1839 and studied at Trinity College, Cambridge, from 1840 to 1845. Always a brilliant scholar, he began writing upon his return to America, at times under the pseudonym of Carl Benson. His essay on the Scots reveals a wide acquaintance with their work, and—when we recall that one of the associative principles was alliteration—a conscious sense of humor (something so rare in this whole body of writing that we begin to fathom almost in wonder its sacred depth of seriousness). The Scottish school have an "analytic manner," he says, and a "(perhaps) consequent synthetic incapacity or indisposition."[116] Contending that all the Scottish writers "are essentially essayists and critics; nothing more," Bristed characterizes "the shrewd, sagacious Reed, the father of their philosophy," as "but the critic of Locke. The desultory and more imaginative Beattie," he continues,

wrote whole volumes of essays, 'good, bad, and indifferent' . . . . Stewart himself—the clear, classic, comprehensive Stewart—was but the Addison of philosophic criticism. The clever, though rather crabbed and conceited Kaims, has given us clusters of critiques and essays, which he dignifies, however, with the titles of "Theory of History," the "Elements of Criticism," the "History of Human Nature" . . . . What are the Lectures of Brown— that subtlest of those proverbs of subtlety, the Scotch metaphysicians—but the essays of a Professor, their elaborate redundancy of phrase and explication, ever on the strain to "*fix*" the volatile essence of his painfully refined analysis, and ever missing it without the clumsy contrivance of his frequent italization.

Thomas Campbell is "the representative of the critical species," another essayist "muffled in the stole of the philosopher."[117]

It seems to me very likely that Bristed is playing on the word *essay* throughout his article to suggest ineptness on the part of the Scots: they are essayers; "essentially" they are those who attempt something, a group of writers who try. And when he wonders if their analytic manner results in a *consequent* lack of synthesis, he may well be having his joke at the expense of Brown's antecedent and invariable-consequent notion of causality. The burden of Bristed's argument, however, is that the critical techniques of the Scots are not suited to the criticism of romantic literature. He prefers Hazlitt, Coleridge, and Carlyle, with their "wild strokes of nature," to Kames and Campbell with their "canons and categories."[118] (By reaching out as he does for hard "c" sounds, Bristed uses an associative principle against the Scots to suggest the rigidity of their thought.) His point is, of course, well taken. Bristed is dissenting from the critical implications and principles of Scottish thought not in the name of society but in the name of literary criticism. Writing from outside the framework of Samuel Gilman and Alexander H. Everett and others, he calls for a new basis for criticism in America; the Scots, he feels, have been holding criticism back; they are responsible for a rigid and monolithic approach to the critical act. Bristed knows who and what stands in the way of legitimate criticism as he sees it, whom and what he must attack. His argument constitutes one more piece of evidence that a freer, more unrestricted form of inquiry, whether philosophical or critical (employing perhaps "wild strokes of nature"), depended on breaking from the safe and stabilizing principles of Common Sense philosophy.

The articles of Everett and Bristed tell us by indirection of the impact of Common Sense thought in America; they mark the boundaries, as I have suggested, of Scottish influence by making us aware of other tendencies, other lines of influence. But the lengthy review of Levi Frisbie's *Inaugural Address* in the *North American Review* (January, 1818) endorses Common Sense philosophy as a kind of American orthodoxy, allowing us to see how the special quality of its conservatism served the needs of American society. Only by understanding this can we understand adequately the hold that Common Sense thought achieved on the American mind. Summing up and bringing into focus the crucial concerns and dominant attitudes of American society, the review becomes representative in a manifold sense.

The reviewer begins by congratulating Americans on the "rapid improvement" of American literature, owing in part to the high quality of popular addresses which bring credit both to the speaker and his audience. Frisbie's address, "though pronounced before the University in Cambridge," he considers "a *popular address*," and it is for this reason that he is "directing the public attention to it."[119] The review begins, therefore, by emphasizing the public nature of an address: the address is for society; it requires an audience (society); and even the structure of the physical setting— one talking to many—suggests that some form of truth is being dispensed. Reviewing Frisbie's address increases the audience by making it available to all who could not personally attend, by making it more public. The reviewer's function is to select from the text and write a commentary, as it were, emphasizing what he considers to be the essential points of social orthodoxy.

Frisbie's subject, we immediately see, lends itself fully to such a treatment. He will speak of "the necessity, the objects, and the influence of Moral Philosophy, in the most extensive sense of the term." Considering first the "moral sense," he defines the basic problem of the human condition: we do not and cannot possess a pure, natural, untainted moral sense. Philosophy is therefore necessary to bring back the perverted judgment and corrupted heart "to the unbiased dictates of nature and common sense."[120] The great danger to man, however, lies in false philosophy presented as a rule of life. Frisbie then invokes a metaphor which contains in one form a recurrent image in the philosophical-critical writing of the time, the image of ideas sifting down from an abstract to what we might call a lived state: "While . . . these speculations of false philosophy are wrapped in metaphysical subtleties, they may excite little alarm, and serve rather to amuse the learned; they are those eccentric lightnings, that play harmlessly in the evening cloud; but when they are made the maxims of common life, or, embodied in popular fiction, find their way into the hearts of men, they are these same lightnings concentrated and brought down to earth, blasting and consuming." Ideas, that is, have consequences; one must diligently distinguish between the true and false ideas that come his way. Frisbie puts it in unequivocal terms. "The safety of society then requires," he says, "that such systems be subjected to the jealous scrutiny of a sound philosophy, and that there be men, whose habits and studies will lead them to a rigid superintendence of whatever is proposed;—to give authority to truth, and to detect and expose what is only specious and insinuating." If our moral being breathed only the pure atmosphere of truth, it might, unaided, preserve soundness of health; "but pampered, as it is, with false philosophy and factitious sentiment, the antidote should grow with the poison. There will always be a Hobbes, a Rousseau, or a Godwin; let us then have also our Cudworths, our Butlers, and our Stewarts."[121]

The judicial quality of Frisbie's remarks is clear and significant; equally significant is the reviewer's praise of what he has quoted from Frisbie: for both men, what is fundamentally at stake in philosophy is the moral basis of the social order. As the first Alford Professor at Harvard, Frisbie is not only a guardian of society, but the trainer of future guardians; and he is calling unequivocally for *moral* guardians. We begin to see the importance of the reviewer's initial stress on the popular and public nature of this address.

Frisbie believes that the moral sense is capable of development; moral knowledge, he says, has not reached its limits. Future moral progress will come from the study of "moral science," which—importantly—will not be confined to the philosopher or student alone. "The same views," he says with emphatic social awareness, "will be gradually applied in the formation of the dispositions and habits of children; they will become an important branch of liberal knowledge, and thus exert a control over the higher classes of society, over men of letters and the popular authors of the day."[122] And from the "popular authors of the day" the "same views" will gradually filter down to the great mass of readers. Again we notice the recurrent image, the basic structure of which is a hierarchical social order in which ideas work their way down from the top, filtering from one level to the next always to the "mass" at the bottom. That the hierarchy is not one of class in the ordinary and established sense of the term is obvious. Indeed, it is difficult to say precisely what kind of hierarchy is implied—an intellectual or conceptual hierarchy perhaps comes closest—for the image is a vehicle for talking about the movement of ideas, invoked to sustain and strengthen the existing social order. It is, therefore, an inherently conservative image, not new, of course, but extremely useful to Americans in the early nineteenth century. Few persons could speak or write about the influence of ideas without employing it in some form. Henry Wheaton, for example, speaking at the opening of the New York Athenaeum in 1824, described his generation as an age of intellectual exertion and power: "Never before did literary men exercise so great an influence over public opinion." Success and prosperity for America, he concludes, depend on the supremacy of the mind, the cultivation of the intellect, and the diffusion of knowledge and the arts—"not merely to the chosen few, but to that immense multitude who are at once invested with the privileges of Freedom and prerogatives of Power."[123]

After illustrating the moral influence of literature—for good and for bad—Frisbie concludes by recommending "the incorporating of religion with morality," for "this extends to every order in society. It is not the fountain, which plays only in the gardens of the palace, but the rain of heaven, which descends alike upon the enclosures of the rich and the poor, and refreshes the meanest shrub, no less than the fairest flower." For Frisbie the idea of perfectibility is a snare, a visionary dream;

but it does not follow, that because every thing is not to be hoped, therefore nothing is to be attempted. Man has certainly capacities of improvement, and he can feel a moral influence; his progress may be fluctuating and slow; but from the application of judicious and unremitting efforts, will it not be certain? Commencing with those, who labour to unfold the principles and ends of moral action, may it not be expected to descend, as we have said, through the higher and more intellectual classes of society, till it reaches and purifies the great mass of mankind in the humblest walks of life; as the blood, flowing from the heart and distributed through the larger arteries, finds its way at length into the capillary and minuter vessels, where it is incorporated with the very substance of the body, giving health and vigour and beauty.[124]

The ultimate influence of ideas on the public has thus the inevitability of physiological process.

Although we cannot be perfect, although we have moral limits, we must progress with "judicious and unremitting efforts" for we know that we have not reached these limits. Frisbie concludes his address, which has been in strict accord, conceptually, with Common Sense thought, with a final insistence on the social meaning of ideas. From such an address I think we can make a necessary distinction between Scottish thought as it existed in the books of Reid, Stewart, Kames, Alison, and Brown and as it existed in the minds of Americans. Primarily it is a distinction in social emphasis (which is to say that the difference lies in what Americans did with Scottish philosophy). Not that the Scots were unconcerned with the social dimensions of their philosophy. In a sense that is why Reid began it all; and the social aspect is of great importance in the thought of both Stewart and Kames. But Americans could apply this body of thought directly and immediately to America; they would convert theory into practice. And once applied and made practical, it would work so well that it would provide a rationale for almost everything Americans wanted to be known for: soberness, security, and safety; but also progress, prosperity, and promise. Perhaps most important of all, it would allow Americans to dream of the future without being visionary, enlisting even such dreams—controlled and made safe—in support of the desired stability.

Frisbie's remarks set off a rhapsodic celebration of America on the part of the reviewer: "There is particular reason," he writes, that the idea of moral progress should "engage and fix our attention." For in America, "mankind seem to be subjected to an experiment to determine their power of improvement, instituted under circumstances incomparably more favourable than ever before existed." Then, the reviewer enumerates the reasons for the happy state of America. "No people," he maintains, "ever entered the high way to honour with such encouragements and advantages":

We are free from any of those institutions transmitted to us from past ages, by which other nations are enthralled, and held back, and allied to the ignorance and vices of their progenitors. The mind is not with us crippled and deformed by prejudices.... We have none of those privileged orders, which are so apt to become stagnant pools of corruption, diffusing moral infection through a people. We acknowledge no claims to superiority, but those which nature has sanctioned, or which are the necessary result of civil society. We have no established church to oppress and bear down the truth. . . .

In short, "we are favoured beyond all example; almost beyond any previous imagination of what might possibly be attained."[125]

It would be difficult to find a passage which brings together more of the fundamental attitudes and beliefs of early American society. Let us note that the reviewer proceeds by negation, that he tells Americans what they are not, what they do not have; he is congratulating Americans on their freedom from the past. The passage prefigures later statements by Margaret Fuller, James Fenimore Cooper, Nathaniel Hawthorne, and Henry James, who in describing the America of the 1830's and 40's employed the same negative rhetoric (in each case, however, with a degree of unfavorable meaning). And it is symptomatic of the total attitude toward the nation at this time: Americans seemed very sure of what they were not; they rejoiced, in fact, at what they were not; instinctively, they shied away from trying to know what they were.[126] First and foremost they wanted to be free of the past, to start over again; to have a new start was to be "favoured beyond all example," for who else could have a new start? The French Revolution had demonstrated the folly of attempting a new start (complete with a new calendar) in an old world; what was needed was a new world, which was, happily, exactly what Americans had.[127]

It is, I believe, precisely because Americans defined themselves negatively that they caught so hungrily at such a conservative body of thought as Common Sense philosophy. For when all the negatives were postulated and applauded, one had finally to consider what was left; and the American self-image was not at all that of an infant nation. A new start did not mean a primitive start.[128] Americans were concerned to start afresh as adults. In Scottish thought they could find a convenient argument for congratulating themselves on escaping a cultural childhood. Moreover, Scottish philosophy provided them with a moral rationale for conservatism when they were bereft of other traditional rationales. It stabilized, it was safe, it discouraged undue speculation, it could be applied to society as a cohesive force. One who went to school to the Scottish philosophers could become the curious anomaly America required—a man, untrammeled by the past, whose essential concern was to conserve the social order. Almost, we might say, a conservative with nothing to conserve; yet that is the paradox at the center of the American experience, a paradox made much more plausible by Common Sense thought. Frisbie's reviewer can boast of the "domestick virtue" and the "high standard of morals" in America. With no institutions of "past ages," no prejudices to cripple and deform the mind, no privileged orders, no hereditary superiority, and no established church, America is stripped clean right down to its virtue. But the reviewer knows that it is possible to be grown-up and civilized without the machinery of civilization; knowing this, he can suggest the means of future improvement.

"Our moral and intellectual condition may be still further improved," he says, by the "diffusion of correct tastes, sentiments, and opinions" of literary men and scholars. "The literature which we want is effective, practical, useful literature, the literature of the intellect and the heart. The men, whom we particularly need, are those, who may guide and form publick opinion and sentiment in matters of taste, in morals, in politicks, and in religion; men, who will think and write like the author of the address, which we have been reviewing."[129] With this explicit call for judicial guidance and criticism of various kinds, for men who will be trained to stand guard over the best interests of society, the reviewer prepares to conclude on a prophetic note. The tone of the following passage is familiar, for there are a number of such passages in early American books and periodicals. In the context of this review, however, such a paean to the future shows us that from the principles of Scottish thought shared by Frisbie and the reviewer could come a belief in the future greatness of America; not only did the philosophy of Common Sense protect the present and more than make up for the loss of the past; it allowed an unlimited hope for the future. It served the needs of Americans by taking care of their hopes as well as their fears. The reviewer concludes by telling his readers that hope for the future entails responsibility in the present:

Never in all past ages did a prospect so glorious rise to the view of any nation, as that which is disclosed to our own. Before some of those who may read what we are now writing, shall taste of death, fifty or sixty millions of men will have poured themselves over our country, carrying civilization and the arts to the extreme corner, where the last of our lakes meet the Mississippi; and making the wilderness disappear before them, and ascending and passing the Rocky Mountains, where the Missouri has its source. The character and condition of this immense multitude depend upon nothing so much as upon the principles and feelings, which may be transmitted to them from the present generation. We ought to acknowledge the debt which is due to our posterity; and to feel that there is no responsibility more solemn, than that of those, who may in any considerable degree affect the destinies of such a people.[130]

In Summary

In surveying the place of Common Sense philosophy in America, we have seen that such men as Franklin, Jefferson, and James Wilson in the eighteenth century respected those of its principles they knew, that gaining an academic foothold at Princeton it spread through the curriculum of American colleges until it achieved what we might call an unofficial status of orthodoxy in the first half of the nineteenth century. Colleges employed as texts the books of Reid, Stewart, Kames, Blair, and Brown, but also—and increasingly—American abridgements or versions of these books. Under teachers who favored the principles of the Scottish school, writers such as Bryant, Emerson, Thoreau, and Lowell, and critics such as Prescott, Gilman, and Walsh studied logic, moral philosophy, and ethics—and the fact that the teachers and writers were sometimes critics added a homogeneity to the total effect. Opponents of Scottish thought took due cognizance of the hold it had on the American mind, a hold best explained by its ability to serve as an apologetic philosophy and by the fact that its principles could be applied to the social order as a stabilizing influence. To recall the words of I. Woodbridge Riley, Common Sense philosophy allowed Americans to "mark time." Increasingly, however, individuals not content to mark time indefinitely began to break away, striving for freer, more unrestricted, less canonical approaches to truth and reality: James Marsh, Emerson, Thoreau, and Charles Astor Bristed, among others, all saw a need to attain a higher than Common Sense truth.

This is, of course, to explain the existence of Scottish realism in America in general terms. In the following chapters I shall attempt to show specifically how the metaphysical principles of Common Sense thought supported a predisposition of the American mind to be suspicious of imaginative experience, how these principles lay behind the prevailing attitude toward fiction in America, and how that attitude in turn prepared the way for the rise of the American "romance." We have seen something of the way in which Americans assimilated the philosophy of Common Sense, how they put it to work in their most serious causes. If it can be characterized as a "moral sedative," we can observe that it was self-prescribed by a society that desired the very latest in sedation. But in helping to mold moral concerns into certain set public patterns, Common Sense thought cast additional suspicion on the area of imaginary or possible experience. Sure of what was real, Common Sense metaphysics had no doubt about what was not real. As we shall see, it defined the real as the actual, contributing in its own way a new dimension to the American distrust of imaginative experience. And nowhere was it of more assistance (or perhaps, ultimately, of more significance) than in strengthening the case against fiction.

2

AMERICAN FICTION AND THE
METAPHYSICS OF ACTUALITY

Chapter Two

ALTHOUGH criticism of the novel in early America varies in degree of intensity, in method, and in motivation, it reveals a remarkable unity of kind. Adverse, dyslogistic, it defines hostility of attitude as the accepted mode for discussion of the novel. Most critics warned readers of the dangers of novel-reading, but not all warnings were delivered in the same way or in the same tone. Much of this hostile criticism, an impressive array of evidence testifying to the case against the novel, has been collected and set forth by Herbert Ross Brown, G. Harrison Orians, and Ormond E. Palmer.[1] Significantly, it is for the most part a body of generic criticism, directed not against individual novels but against the novel as a form. And yet it is somehow more than that, too, and we are probably closer to its meaning if we read this criticism as a case against the very idea of fiction, as an argument based ultimately on a mistrust of the imagination.

This is not to overlook or to deny the existence of criticism of individual novels. One has only to examine the lengthy reviews of the novels of Maria Edgeworth, Scott, or Cooper, or the critical notices of little-known early American novels to see that judgment was being passed on individual works and that a novel could earn praise as well as blame. Individual reviews, however, should be seen against the larger backdrop of a generic hostility to the novel (or to fiction)—the full meaning of the former can be derived only from the latter. Out of this paradox that what is true generally is not always true particularly comes a curious anomaly: a critic often bestowed praise on a novel because it was not very much like a novel—because it taught so well, because it was so elevated in tone; and thus, approval of the particular novel becomes censure of the genre. Practically all the praise of Miss Edgeworth's novels operates generically against the novel in this way.

For purposes of clarity, let us describe the novel in traditional terms: as Clara Reeve put it in *The Progress of Romance* (1785), the novel portrays real life and manners and the time in which it is written, whereas the romance "describes what never happened nor is likely to happen." Accordingly, we may take the novel to be a realistic literary form which deals with contemporary life and refer to the realistic mode of representation within that form as *novelistic*. Another important characteristic of the novel is its tendency to allude in some way to a further world of fiction, always as a way of establishing a greater claim of its own to reality. A novel may burlesque extravagant fictions (as Cervantes first demonstrated) or it may contain scenes in which a character momentarily and subtly sees his situation as resembling fiction.[2] In either case the novel's reality (or the sense of reality in the novel) is augmented at the expense of the inner or second or dependent fiction it sustains, for this dependent fiction is automatically made to seem more ethereal, less real, by the simple expedient of referring to it. When a husband (in a novel) tells his wife to stop acting like a character in a novel, our sense of his reality increases because he can make the same distinction (between actuality and fiction) that we can make—and the terms of novelistic representation encourage him to do so. And in a novel about a novelist, the career of the novelist will seem more real than the novels he is supposed to be writing. For the same reason, the novel may make excellent use of the framework device: the framework will be novelistic—contemporary, often domestic—while the inner fiction will be more extravagant. A group of English gentlemen may thus gather in the library after dinner and, over cordials, listen to one of their number relate a tale of werewolves in Transylvania. But it never happens the other way around. The novel, by virtue of its resources, may be aware of the romance, or of itself, but the romance lacks the technical resources to be aware of either.

Unfortunately, but significantly enough, many early American critics of fiction did not observe the distinction between the novel and the romance with any regularity (though it was there to be observed); either they did not know of it or it sometimes failed to signify because of the scope of their mistrust of fiction. To writers of fiction, however, the distinction seems to have been important; they used the terms *novel* and *romance*, and they used them correctly. It may seem ironic that the general mistrust of fiction would ultimately be felt most strongly, as we shall see, in novelistic creation; but, then, the novel's stance of reality was a pseudo-stance, and it was very possible defensively to insist on "reality" to the detriment of one's fiction.

My concern here will be with the generic criticism of the novel, and with the assumptions and implications of this criticism. Mr. Brown, Mr. Orians, and Mr. Palmer have demonstrated the quantitative existence of an anti-novel attitude; I shall attempt to examine its qualitative mode by presenting selected examples of criticism which will provide material for analyzing the rationale of the criticism as a whole.

The Case Against Fiction

To assess and appreciate this body of adverse criticism for what it was, one must understand that these critics were intensely—at times, grimly—serious about what they wrote. This may appear to be an unnecessary reminder, but it will seem less so if we recall the changes in thought and attitude from one century to the next. The first reaction of a twentieth-century reader on learning that the bulk of early American criticism on the subject of the novel regarded that form as a potential tool of immorality, as something dangerous to one's moral and intellectual well-being, would be to laugh at the idea and at the simple-minded people who held it—this despite the fact that our popular "novel" today contains much that is anti-novelistic and draws fire for serving as a vehicle for self-indulgence. Living, as we do, in a society in which the novel is the dominant literary form, we must make an effort of mind to get in touch with such criticism, to see it as its writers saw it, to view it in terms of its own culture. And it is precisely in such terms that we must view this criticism if it is to make any sense at all. If, for special reasons, we cut it apart from its culture, we rob it of its *raison d'être* and lose sight of the fact that it existed as a vital force within a given social milieu.

The tendency to treat this criticism lightly has been fostered and perpetuated by some of those who have dealt with the early American novel and the criticism of that novel. Quite obviously this criticism is amusing; no effort is required to see its (unintentional) humor. But equally obvious should be the fact of its seriousness. My effort will be to take this criticism of the novel seriously, to demonstrate that it had a meaning of its own—an absolutely humorless meaning involving in the final analysis matters of moral life and death.

In 1807 Samuel F. Jarvis, two years out of Yale College, delivered an "oration. . . , before the society of PHI BETA KAPPA, upon the anniversary of that institution." After calling for a system of government-sponsored patronage to promote the cause of American literature, Jarvis turns his attention to the reading habits of the American people. He finds that "the whole extent of their reading is comprehended in productions of the imagination." In particular, "the taste for Novels and all other kinds of light reading has risen to an astonishing and alarming height. Like the lean kine of Pharaoh, they have swallowed up all other reading, and like them too, they have not looked the better for it." The true cause for alarm, however, rests not in the simple fact that novels are read; rather, it lies in "the evil consequences attendant upon novel reading," which are "much greater than has generally been imagined." Few writers, continues Jarvis, "who forge a series of events," consider the responsibility they assume and the particular hazard attached to their undertaking. Since the writers (and the events) lack truth as their basis, "they are continually liable to give false notions of things, to pervert the consequences of human actions, and to misrepresent the ways of divine providence." For the ways of men, "so far as they are passive under the consequences of their own actions, are the ways of God."[3]

Jarvis does not state categorically that novels are immoral. His opposition to fiction takes a much more devastating turn, however, when he questions the effects of "productions of the imagination" and presents his arguments in terms of moral responsibility. Jarvis distrusts the imagination and hence the novel. To him, the novel is not a plaything with which to idle away an hour. Rather, it is an invention of insidious potency; for in a novel one finds the author undertaking the terrible responsibility of playing God, of creating a little world and the people in it, of having them act for good and for evil, and of meting out rewards and punishments in the light of a mortal and hence fallible mind. No matter the innocent and honorable intention of the novelist; he is continually liable "to misrepresent the ways of divine providence." For how can a man with impunity take over the role of God, even temporarily? The novel, lacking truth as its basis, is by that very fact unable to correspond with the eternal, timeless plan of God. As a substitute, it is based on the particular plan of a particular man. In short, the novel substitutes the finite for the infinite, the temporal for the eternal, the fallible for the infallible—man as creator for God as Creator.[4] Small wonder that it is full of danger and prone to error. Small wonder that Jarvis views it as something liable to have evil consequences; for, as the steady reading diet of a society, the novel could prove a menace to the entire moral order. Thus, in a very real sense, Jarvis' criticism of the novel can be viewed as a defense of the existing moral order; the tone of his remarks is as serious as if he were defending the existence of God, on which that order depended.

Jarvis admits in a footnote that he is indebted to the Reverend William Jones of Nayland for the idea he has been developing. And in his *Letters from a Tutor to His Pupil*, the English clergyman speaks to the same problem. Very often, writes Jones, historical circumstances tempt men to question the justice of God; to write a series of fictitious events is to operate at a farther remove—for in fiction the circumstances themselves are man-made and not God-made. A writer may mean well, admits Jones, and yet through error may place virtue in circumstances of distress such as Providence "never did nor will, and thereby may bring discouragements upon virtue, and even throw it into despair." Quite without intention, a writer may attribute to vice a success "which it never had, nor will have, so long as God

governs the world."[5] Here again it is the novelist's prone-
ness to error and the role he would assume that motivate
the objection to novels. The English and American clerics
agree fully (though the homiletic tone of the English conduct book contrasts with the more intellectualized didacticism of the American Phi Beta Kappa address): no amount
of moral integrity can make a man anything but a man. The
only true, unsuspect novel would be one written by God.

Both the manner of Jarvis' statement regarding fiction
and the kind of idea he has borrowed from Jones are worthy
of note. We see immediately that this is not shrill, irresponsible criticism; Jarvis uses none of the devices of hysteria
and makes little or no play on the sensational, as did some
of those who attacked the novel. His special vehicle of
attack is a belief, deeply held, confidently formulated. He
proceeds quietly, not casting blame but calling attention to
the obvious and assumed fact of man's imperfection and the
consequences of that imperfection. There is no need to
prove that man is fallible, no need to argue that man is liable
to error; Jarvis assumes man's imperfection and starts from
that fact as from a common undebatable ground. Indeed, the
rhetoric of debate is no part of Jarvis' statement. And there
is no quality of contention in the idea that he has adopted
from Jones: God is the true Creator. The implications of
that credo constitute the special power of Jarvis' opposition
to fiction. This kind of instruction must have been familiar
to his readers, who may have been hearing it every Sunday,
but it is now being recalled and applied to novels. He can
afford to employ a simplicity both of message and rhetoric.
Only in his pejorative metaphor alluding to "the lean kine
of Pharaoh," appropriated, incidentally, from Jones, does he
attempt open disparagement. Intensely serious, he can proceed without bombast because he is on sure ground.

A far more extended and equally sober examination into

the dangers of reading novels is that conducted by the Reverend Dr. James Gray in an address on "female education" in 1810. Dr. Gray's remarks are especially pertinent here, I believe, for in 1793 he graduated from the University of Glasgow, where he knew Thomas Reid; according to a contemporary, he "entertained the most unqualified respect" for Reid.[6] He thus embodies a direct Common Sense influence in early nineteenth century America. Arriving in the United States in 1797, Dr. Gray became a significant figure in the Associate Reformed Church, assisting importantly in the establishment of its Theological Seminary in New York, helping to form the Philadelphia Bible Society in 1808, and founding schools in Philadelphia and Baltimore.[7] Extremely well formulated, his discussion of the novel constitutes the most thorough and searching analysis I have discovered from the point of view of one whose philosophic credo was Common Sense philosophy. The occasion of Dr. Gray's remarks is a convocation of students and friends of the "Philadelphia Academy for the Instruction of Young Ladies"; his role is that of trustee. After recommending "biography, history, and works of religion and morals" as suitable future reading for the students, he turns his attention to what they should not read:

There is a species of composition, young ladies, which were I not to mention on such an occasion as the present, the omission might be considered a studied one, and perhaps censured as improper. You already anticipate the mention of novels. I am aware that the theme is trite. I might begin by indulging a sharp invective against the general class of such books; I might then except a few from the general censure; and afterwards proceed to inquire whether more good or evil accrues to society from such reading. But why consume the hour. The books are written and will be read.[8]

The self-interest of authors, printers, and booksellers and the "passions of the youthful heart" force novels onto the market.

Dr. Gray's introductory remarks indicate that there is an expected pattern of remarks on the subject of novels. He knows that the subject is "trite"; he knows, too, that he must say something, for society and morality are involved. Having announced that he will not attack the novel directly, he proceeds with skillful rhetoric and dialectic to analyze the "advantages" which may be expected from the reading of novels, "allowing the selection to be made with the greatest possible judgment and felicity, and wholly overlooking any injury which they may be supposed to inflict on the mental constitution." Gray believes that it is impossible "to state the question in terms more liberal and generous." I should like to quote the entire pertinent section of Gray's analysis, for the cogency of the argument depends to a large extent on totality of effect. Indeed, the full power of this entire body of criticism hostile to the novel is diluted by the extraction of well formulated phrases or sentences to serve as examples; Gray's remarks, in particular, require to be read in the original and in full.

When we hear novels celebrated as means for teaching young people the knowledge of human nature, we seem to perceive in the language something so ambiguous and undefined, something which needs so much commentary and qualification, that, like the gordian knot it is better to cut it at once than to waste time in unravelling its complications. I say, therefore, when we shall see great orators formed by silent meditation, and great anatomists formed by the study of copperplate skeletons and dissections, then, and not till then, shall we behold judges of human life and character produced by novel reading. To study human nature you must mix with mankind: it is in the drawing

room, not in the library, in the forum, not in the cloister, that
the nature of man can be learned, because it is in the former
places, not in the latter, that it is displayed in its true colours
and proportions. However narrow the circle of individual feeling and experience may be, it comprises almost the whole of
what any person knows of this subject: and no extent of genius
and learning can supply the want of a practical acquaintance
with society. The only accession which our experimental
knowledge on this subject admits, is derived from authentic
history. If it be asked, May not novels supply the place of history? May they not exhibit views of human nature not found
in history? And may they not exhibit more perfect instances of
virtue and vice than any that occur in real life? To the two
latter interrogations I answer, that these perfect characters, are
only perfect monsters. They go to mislead. They can do no
good. That extravagance of vice which does not occur in real
life can never answer the purpose of deterring us from vitious
indulgence; and virtues which have never been practised can
scarcely become examples. As to the other interrogatory, the
answer is obvious, that to supplant a reality by a fiction is a
preposterous method of diffusing truth. But I would ask, is
human nature really adequate to the production of a consistent
human character by the creations of fancy? Certainly to mark
the reigning passion, to delineate the fixed and prevailing habits,
to limit or aid their operation by various whims and caprices,
to conceive and arrange the events and objects which operate
on all these powers; to ascertain, amidst the collisions of con-
flicting principles, and to arrest and fix those nice shades which
give congruity to character, is, to say the least, no easy task; a
task perhaps beyond the reach of man. A few rare men there
have been, I grant, who have achieved great things in characteristic moral painting, still they have not come up to nature. Let
us praise them as we do those sculptors who exhibit a few striking points in the human figure; and if they have not been able
to bid the heart beat, and the tongue speak, and the features
move, let us pardon their failure because the thing was impossible.

There is, however, only one idea about which I feel any great solicitude. Permit me to caution you against ever making the characters of romance a standard by which to judge of character in real life. For be assured that the sir Guys and madam Bridgets, the Lotharios and Matildas of the novelists are very different personages, from the men and women with whom it has pleased God to people this world. And perhaps it may be found that no persons are more apt to err and blunder, when introduced on the stage of real life than those whose imaginations have been deeply impressed with the characters of fictitious composition.

Another allegation in favour of novels, is that they contribute to the cultivation of sensibility; and render us more sympathetic, more disposed to weep with those who weep, and rejoice with those who rejoice; and of consequence dispose us to receive the calamities which occur in the human condition; and are on the whole subservient to virtue. I confess I feel stronger doubts on this subject than on the foregoing. I am not satisfied that the theory is verified by fact, or corresponds with the essential laws of our nature. There can be no doubt that novels act extensively on our feelings, and are able to rob us of many a sob and many a tear. They are a species of artificial stimulant. But it is very questionable whether these chamber cordials are really conducive to the health of our minds; whether this surreptitious enjoyment of our faculties does not rather indispose us to the practical exercise of sympathy in real life. The general sense of mankind on this subject appears not to be obscure; for if any one were in quest of an attentive physician, a tender nurse, or a sympathetic friend, it would not be found an effectual recommendation of any particular person to say that he, or she, was a great reader of novels.

The real advantages of this species of reading appear to be these, that it sometimes creates a taste for reading which continues through life; that it habituates the young mind to the analysis of character; that it imparts a species of sentimental eloquence to conversation; and were I certain that it does not increase the disorder which it is intended to cure, I should apprehend that it may serve as a wastegate to the overflowings of youthful sensibility.

After all, the season for indulging this species of mental diversion is very transient. It is during the vernal equinox of our existence, when the sun is passing the line which separates childhood from maturity, a period when all is tumult in the human constitution, that the fictions of romance claim a natural dominion over us, only because the mind is then itself the region of fiction, of hopes and fears, of plans and projects, far beyond the narrow limits of sober reality. But in proportion as it grows up to maturity, and as the grand prospects of society expand to its view, it becomes incapable of being roused to action by anything but what is real; it flings away the pap and syllabub of fiction, and calls for more substantial food. This is certainly the natural course of things.

Ghosts, goblins and enchanted castles, do for children; Masters and Misses are enraptured with the sentimental novel; but, unless a morbid taste for fiction be contracted, or the growth of mind be stunted for a want of nutriment, men and women demand fact and doctrine. And provided a taste for the sacred doctrines has been contracted at any period of life, when a man approaches the verge of earthly being, and his sun begins to dip in the western wave, nothing can suffice his mind but those sublime and substantial compositions. In this remark I do not confine my views to a Boyle or a Locke, and a few other very rare, because very great characters. The doctrine is general: it is a law of our nature. For it I may be allowed to borrow a phrase from the medical gentlemen, our minds, like our bodies, act by the continual impression of stimulants; and as the fibre waxes rigid, you must increase the stimulating power.

The passage is undeniably powerful. As he raises every conceivable argument in favor of the novel, Gray proceeds to undercut each one with doubts, with dispassionate logic, with references to axiomatic truths. Never does he attempt to carry a point solely by asseveration. His method is at once concessive and argumentative; concessive because he knows his audience and perhaps dares not risk antagonizing the youthful portion with a heavy-handed assault, and, more important, because he believes implicitly that the concessions he makes will not vitiate his essential position; argumentative, because his task is to leave the novel with no positive value, to invalidate the very substance of fiction. His sincerity and seriousness are matched throughout by the degree of his assurance.

Doubly interesting and important is the fact that although Gray's purpose is moral in the sense that it is intended to influence action, he introduces no specific moral sanctions. The inquiry is at bottom epistemological and metaphysical—the crucial issues are those of truth and reality. In the context of Gray's remarks these concepts became two aspects of the same consideration, for in terms of the dichotomy which he sets up the true coincides with the real. Any other opinion is not only unorthodox but positively heretical and fraught with danger. Such a sentence as "to supplant a reality by a fiction is a preposterous method of diffusing truth" suggests the relationship between the two concepts: out of reality one may draw truth; out of non-reality (which is to say a distorted, dislocated reality) one can draw only error.

The crux of the matter is, of course, Gray's definition of reality. Using a disjunctive dialectic structure, he divides things quickly, neatly, and easily into the real and the artificial. His examples (each formulated disjunctively, suggesting cumulatively a possible Ramist influence that would make the structure of his argument fit well with the Puritan intellectual heritage) strengthen the disjunction, which is reflected rhetorically and syntactically. On the one hand he points to what is real—"the drawing room," "the forum"; on the other he describes the artificial—"the library," "the cloister." Applying this dichotomy to the matter under consideration, he summarily divorces the novel from what is real. The novel is artificial, it is a fiction, a *mensonge;* reality is to be found in life as it is actually lived. In Gray's words, "to study human nature you must mix with mankind."

The inherent metaphysical assumption underlying these words is that true reality is limited to the actual, that is, to actually existing being. Gray does not deny the existence of an order of possibly existing being; to do so would be absurd, for one is patently able to imagine that which lacks objective, actual existence. Indeed, this is precisely what the novelist does, and this is precisely how he invents false reality. Reality, then, divides into the actual and the possible, and these two modes of being partake of their existence in distinctly different ways, for in the final analysis one is true and the other false. Life, the totality of one's experience, is actual, is true, and it is the truth of actual experience that enables one to learn from it. A novel, a collection of invented incidents, is possible (artificial), is false, and it is the falseness of possible experience that vitiates any attempt to learn from it. The distinction is imperative: to neglect to make it would be to allow false reality to subvert true reality.

The status or function of the order of possibility is, of course, a crucial problem in all metaphysics. We have seen that Gray conceives of the possible as an order of dark, unreal being, a realm of distortion which will infect the mind of one who dwells too long within its boundaries. It has a limited function as an order of being in which youthful minds may enjoy a fanciful holiday. But Gray is emphatic on the point that it is not the proper order for those of mature mind. Converting a contemporaneous notion of primitivism to his own use, he reasons simply, with the assurance of one who understands that his is the common, the correct view: a child enters only partially into the world of actuality; he lives in a world of parents and superiors who make decisions for him. Hence, there is little harm in permitting what seems to be a natural tendency (natural because the child is not yet ready to cope with the world of actuality)—the exploration of the order of the possible. The period of indulgence, however, is brief. Maturing involves an increasing realization that one's life is to be lived in the actual world (one's entire conditioning will be toward this realization), and so one gradually puts off the artificial things of the child and adopts the truly natural, safe, and practical things of the adult. The adult should enter fully into the world of actuality, should prepare himself to cope with actual problems, actual events, actual people. The world of the possible, the world of youth, is retrogressive and forbidden.

Gray's argument, as suggested above, constitutes an interesting adaptation of the theory that poetry and art belong properly to primitive (what we might call culturally childish) societies, a theory given much attention by Scottish writers in the eighteenth century. Espousing a cultural relativism, such men as Thomas Blackwell, John Robert Scott, and Hugh Blair contended that great art was indigenous to primitive society and, conversely, that one sign of a society's maturity was that it no longer fostered great art. In eighteenth-century England the major function of this esthetic primitivism was to explain why no great art was being created and to celebrate the progress away from the primitive origins of art. Some writers, Kames and Stewart among them, took up anti-primitivistic positions, contending that the imagination in early societies was merely wild and unchecked, powerful, to be sure, but unformed.[9] Whatever one's view of the quality of primitive art, the notion of esthetic primitivism was capable of providing a useful analogue for someone such as Gray, who would equate the imaginative and the childish *personally* and argue that man must leave his childhood (just as society must) if he is to progress. The adult grows away from "the region of fiction" to a higher, better, and necessary reality. Gray's argument admits of no nostalgia; though childhood may be tolerated, it is weak and unprotected and by no means great; man must grow up to view "the grand prospects of society." By means of his extremely effective adaptation, Gray has enlisted the help of anti-primitivism in his attack on the novel. In his terms, and they are the inexorable terms of Common Sense, the novel becomes a childish toy, a latter-day epic to be shunted aside by a mature, enlightened world.

Conceived of in Gray's manner, the order of the possible has no calculable, no predictable relation to the actual order. The disjunction is complete, from the most abstract metaphysical assumption to the very practical advice that Gray offers to the young ladies before him. Deriving as it does from his metaphysical principles, the advice could be predicted: "permit me to caution you against ever making the characters of romance a standard by which to judge of character in real life," and again, "perhaps it may be found that no persons are more apt to err and blunder, when introduced on the stage of real life, than those whose imaginations have been deeply impressed with the characters of fictitious composition." The tone is cautious, undogmatic. Respected and assured, Gray doubtless realizes that he will be more successful if he can convince his auditors that what he says comes from a deep and personal meditation on the subject rather than from a blind sharing in the common attitude. He strives syntactically to achieve this conviction by qualifying, by cautioning instead of forbidding, by being not entirely certain, by feeling strong doubts on a subject, by seeming to perceive, by admitting the word "perhaps" into his discourse. Gray the clergyman, the member of the board of trustees, the respectable citizen of Philadelphia, knows his position, knows in effect that the formidable distinction which he has set up will be all the stronger for a few rhetorical and syntactical concessions. For what he is saying admits of no ambiguity: a right-minded person will not attempt to apply to the actual order something he has learned from the possible. There is no safe method of transfer; the orders are essentially distinct and different since one is compatible with truth and the other is not. If we ignore this distinction, we run counter to the first principles of metaphysics and confuse the very nature of existence.

It is clear that such a metaphysics places the novel—as a form of fiction—in a completely untenable position. The novel, requiring the use of the possible, by that very fact disassociates itself from truth, from actuality. Were the novel to conform metaphysically, were it to limit itself to the actual, the result would be indistinguishable from history, would in fact be history. For history orders a series of actual events, history relates the successes and failures, the hopes and fears, of actual men, history, as record, is actuality in the form of language. Precisely for this reason Gray and many other critics of the novel encouraged the reading of history as an antidote to novel-reading and as a valuable and admirably safe method of extending one's knowledge of reality. The Scottish James Beattie spoke for many Americans when he said that a habit of reading fiction "breeds a dislike for history."[10] These men share in what Crane Brinton calls "the general verdict of our Western civilization," the idea that "a knowledge of history is at the very least a kind of extension of individual experience, and is therefore of value to the human intelligence that makes use of experience." But Mr. Brinton also calls history "a most useful guide in the formation of common sense." It is not "a worker of miracles. If you want miracles—certainly a very human want—you must look elsewhere than to history."[11] The statement offers a lucid presentation of the issue facing a society that did not want miracles or the risk of miracles. History for such a society conforms to common sense; it derives from a sense of reality which glorifies the actual and ignores or denigrates (because it fears) the possible; it cannot work miracles. The existence of the novel, on the other hand, depends on its ability to work miracles, to articulate, explore, and give order to the possible. Between history and actual life there exists a one-to-one relationship; only thus can history be construed as an extension of individual experience. Between the novel and actual life, however, there exists no true, no predictable relationship; the novel rises out of the shadowy, distorted order of the possible. Implicit in this distinction is a critical philosophy of history which sees history as open to common-sense study and reconstruction because it happened, while the novel, never having happened, is thereby closed to the same kind of consideration. In the antithesis between the written word as history and the written word as fiction one sees reflected the basic metaphysical antithesis between the actual and the possible.

Not all criticism of the novel was as concessively mild in tone as that of Gray or as simply didactic as that of Jarvis. In his *Brief Retrospect of the Eighteenth Century*, Samuel Miller contends that many novels are so "contemptibly frivolous" that to read them is "a most criminal waste of time."[12] The context of Miller's remarks is a consideration of individual novels which occupies the greater part of his chapter "Romances and Novels." Toward the end of the chapter, however, he treats of novels generically. "There is no species of writing," he says, "which, promiscuously pursued, has a more direct tendency to discourage the acquisition of solid learning, to fill the mind with vain, unnatural, and delusive ideas, and to deprave the moral tastes." Although he judges some novels to be superior to others, even the best "are only fitted to mislead. To fill the mind with unreal and delusive pictures of life, is, in the end, to beguile it from sober duty, and to cheat it from substantial enjoyment." The effects of novel-reading comprise "a mass of misery and crime too great for the ordinary powers of calculation." To read novels "habitually and indiscriminately" is to invite "intellectual and moral ruin."[13]

Miller's belief that to forbid all novel-reading "would be an indiscreet and dangerous extreme" and that therefore it is "not unadvisable" to select a "*very few . . .* of the *best*" for reading appears to be a concession to inevitability. Gray had conceded the same point, that novels would be written, published, and read. In a final footnote, however, Miller has "no hesitation in saying, that, if it were *possible,* he would *wholly* prohibit the reading of novels." Although some novels might not be harmful, one cannot hope that the proper selection will be made "out of the polluted and mischievous mass continually presented to the youthful mind." One must, concludes Miller adamantly, restrain the "gratification" of novel reading "within *small bounds.*" And in words made electric by the use of capitals he pronounces, "with confidence," that "NO ONE WAS EVER AN EXTENSIVE AND ESPECIALLY AN HABITUAL READER OF NOVELS, EVEN SUPPOSING THEM ALL TO BE WELL SELECTED, WITHOUT SUFFERING BOTH INTELLECTUAL AND MORAL INJURY, AND OF COURSE INCURRING A DIMINUTION OF HAPPINESS."[14]

Again we have the same metaphysical assumptions, so devastating to the novel: novels present "unreal and delusive pictures of life" to the reader; they mislead; they discourage one from "solid learning" and "sober duty." And the effects of succumbing to their unreality and delusion are said to be literally terrifying. Again we have reality divided into the

actual and the possible; again we see that everything substantial and sober and right and good is in the actual order,
and that possibility is an order of grave peril, where one runs
the risk of "intellectual and moral ruin." The stress of Miller's remarks is on this intellectual and moral injury, on the
effects of novel-reading. He does not set up a patiently reasoned frame of values from which to attack the novel (as
does Gray), but insists directly and with emphasis on their
danger to one's happiness and well-being. Nonetheless,
despite their differences in tone, manner, and approach, Miller, Gray, and Jarvis share the same metaphysical position.
Though a rhetorical and syntactical affiliation with metaphysical principles is more apparent in Gray's address, Miller's attack on the novel is based ultimately, and just as
certainly, on the primary metaphysical principle that the
order of possibility is delusive, distorted, and dangerous.
This is the true metaphysics, Miller assumes, and he warns
his readers to bring their actions, their lives, their minds,
into conformity with its obviously correct principles.

Defensive Measures

Although both the quantity and quality of hostile feeling
toward the novel appear to have been significant, a few
critics demurred. In such a minority position was Joseph
Dennie, who, as editor of *The Port Folio*, spoke his Fed-
eralist mind clearly, if often unpopularly, on contemporary
political and cultural matters. Dennie never joined in the
chorus which heaped abuse on the novel; the official attitude
of *The Port Folio* toward fiction was more kindly than that
of most other periodicals, and occasionally Dennie himself
came forward as its apologist. In a front-page article in 1807
he discusses the subject of novel-reading. "Novels and romances," he begins,

have been proscribed by many old-fashioned people, not only because they occupy a portion of our time which might be employed to more advantage, but because they are apt to infuse a romantick spirit, to instil sentiments too refined for mere mortals, in short because the novelist creates an imaginary world and brings us acquainted with beings of a superior order, whose actions we are studying when we ought to be observing the motives of those beings by whom we are surrounded, with whom we are obliged to mix, and from whom we are to derive our happiness.

As the first of these reasons here given will apply to almost every species of amusement into which we enter I shall pass it over, merely remarking by the way, that relaxation is as necessary to the vigour of the mind as sleep is to that of the body. Upon the second and most substantial reason I shall dwell somewhat longer. When we have gained a tolerable knowledge of the world, and are somewhat acquainted with the real nature and motives of its inhabitants, works of fiction may be resorted to as an amusement the most dignified, the most worthy of the attention of a rational being—our reason is in no danger of being mislead: for though we may suffer imagination to take the lead for the moment, and to make us spectators of actions the most heroic and sublime, yet we can quit her guidance at pleasure— when we lay down the book our brain becomes cool, the fairy scene vanishes; we remember it as but a pleasant dream, and we return to the contemplation of man, as he is, with a judgment as cool and correct as it was before. In short, in this case that employment of the Imagination is but a refreshing slumber to the Judgment.

But, if before we are acquainted with the real state of things, we make fiction our study—If we suppose we behold in the works of the poet, the picture of unvarnished nature; when we afterwards become acquainted with men we will be sure to behold them with disappointment and perhaps with disgust.[15]

There are two important points to be made in connection with this passage. First of all, Dennie recognizes the issues

at stake; he recognizes the grounds on which opponents of
the novel base their opposition. He is aware that the novel
is commonly regarded as a human creation arisen from the
order of the possible, a creation whose existence might constitute a threat to the order of the actual. And to judge from
the tone of his introductory remarks, Dennie does not believe that he is saying anything new; rather, he appears to
be summarizing the known, taking stock of what is commonly realized, as an introduction to his own remarks which
are to follow. We may thus assume, I believe, that the whole
argument over the novel and its effects would be well known
throughout American society and that the educated popu-
lace, at least, would be familiar with the issues involved and
the terms in which those issues were conventionally formulated.

The second point comes somewhat as a surprise; for
although he is writing in defense of novels, and although he
recognizes the implicit metaphysical position of those who
oppose the novel, Dennie absolutely refuses to attack that
position. Indeed, he allies himself with it; his entire statement
on novel-reading is based on the same metaphysical principles as those of Jarvis, Gray, and Miller. The possible is
still the order of the unreal, the order of half-truth or
un-truth, the order of fictions. Although Dennie does disagree with the other men whose statements I have quoted,
his disagreement is irrelevant to their basic argument. Dennie posits a mature, rightly formed mentality with a firm
hold on actuality, and maintains that this mentality has nothing to fear from (occasional) novel-reading. Not because
the novel as purveyor of possibility is not dangerous; as an
ordered sequence of possible events it is indeed perilous
reading. Dennie believes, however, that this hypothetical
adult mentality can return from its fictional explorations
"with a judgment as cool and correct as it was before,"

which is to say, the reader will return the same as he (or she) was before reading any particular novel. (It is obvious that the reader must return; for a right-minded person, a person with a sure grasp of reality, there is no alternative.) Thus the novel offers nothing in any way positive or negative or lasting; the reader brings back from his adventure nothing which he can apply, or should want to apply, to the world of actuality, nothing that he can hold in his mind and utilize in the real world. The novel affords "a refreshing slumber to the Judgment"; it is a harmless because ineffectual recreation. This, then, is the difference: the novel to Dennie has no effects, good or evil, beyond the immediate impressions of the moment; the novel to Gray (or Jarvis or Miller) has decidedly dangerous and lingering evil effects. Gray believes that readers of the novel might somehow—perhaps involuntarily—attempt a transfer from the actual to the possible; such an attempt, running counter to the most primary of metaphysical principles, would be foredoomed to a failure which might take any one of a number of evil forms. Dennie would agree that were any such transfer to be made, it would be exceedingly perilous, but for his mature novel-reader there is simply no question of transfer. He returns to "the contemplations of man, as he is," unchanged. The dichotomy between the orders of the actual and possible has become absolute.

The fiction written in a society which conceived of reality in such terms would naturally be affected in certain ways. We may assume that novelists, in differing degrees, would share the common attitude and that one of their simplest means of writing fiction and remaining metaphysically (and morally) orthodox would be to claim a factual basis for their work, to pass it off as true. Such claims are, as we know, characteristic of the early American novel. For example, *The Power of Sympathy* (1789) claims to be

Founded in Truth; The Hapless Orphan (1793) is *Founded on Incidents in Real Life;* the well known *Charlotte Temple* (1794) is *A Tale of Truth; The Coquette* (1797) is *Founded on Fact;* both *Amelia, or the Faithless Briton* (1798) and *Julia and the Illuminated Baron* (1800) are *Founded on Recent Facts;* while *The Last Resource, or Female Fortitude* (1809) is *Founded on Recent Facts in the Western Parts of Pennsylvania.*

In prefaces, too, the novelist could show his awareness of the dangers of fiction and avail himself of the time-honored device of claiming authenticity. The clamorous insistence on authenticity, however, betrays the kind and degree of seriousness with which these authors went about their work; it is more than the mere invoking of a literary device. Mrs. Martha Read, for example, disclaims membership in "the honorable tribe of Novel-Tinkers"; her *Monima; or, the Beggar Girl* (1802) is "founded on fact." In the preface to the second edition of *Monima* in the following year, Mrs. Read complains that her "veracity has been boldly called into question, in regard to the truth" of the novel. It is her "sacred opinion" that her critics have never read *Monima*, but know of it only "through the medium of report or prejudice." "But I do solemnly aver," she concludes, "that the tale of MONIMA is founded on facts."[16] In *Lucinda; or, the Mountain Mourner* (1807), by Mrs. P. D. Manvill, we find a startling and unique *apologia:* a number of respectable citizens have signed the following testimonial letter, which prefaces the novel. "To the Publick":

We, the undersigned, having perused the book entitled "Lucinda, or the Mountain Mourner," &c. recommend it to the attention of the American publick, and particularly to the young and inexperienced, as possessing, from its being founded on realities, superior merit to most publications of a similar nature. It contains, according to the best information, (and some of us are thoroughly acquainted with many of the circumstances therein recorded,) a narrative statement of the most *incontestable facts,* and is well calculated to afford not only amusement, but useful instruction, to every reader of sensibility and reflection.[17]

In neither of these cases is the manner one of levity; these are not elaborate literary jokes. Mrs. Read gives her "sacred" opinion and avers "solemnly." Mrs. Manvill has the protection of what amounts to a multiple imprimatur; what she calls the "sacred truths" of her novel have been judged by responsible members of society, and blessed; indeed, judicial criticism, in the most literal sense, has been rendered in this case before the sale of the book.

Perhaps more typical as a preface is that introducing Sukey Vickery's *Emily Hamilton* (1803). Miss Vickery admits that novel-reading "is frequently mentioned as being in the highest degree prejudicial to young minds, by giving them wrong ideas of the world, and setting their tastes so high as to occasion a disrelish for those scenes in which they are necessitated to take a part." An "early attachment" to novels has in truth ruined many persons, she continues. Not all novels, however, should be condemned:

Those which carry us too far from real life, and fill the imagination with a thousand enchanting images which it is impossible ever to realize, conveying at the same time an idea of perfect earthly happiness, ought never to be read till the judgment is sufficiently mature to separate the truth from the fiction of the story. But those which are founded on interesting scenes in real life, may be calculated to afford moral instruction to the youthful mind, in the most pleasing manner.[18]

These statements show an awareness of the issues involved in novel-writing and novel-reading. Unable, and perhaps unwilling, to refute the charge that novel-reading is prejudicial (in the "highest respect") to "young minds," Miss Vickery concedes that many persons have been ruined by such reading. And it is the "erroneous ideas" derived from novels that prepare one's downfall. Again we meet the same metaphysical principles and assumptions; Miss Vickery plays down the role of possibility in her novel and in good novels generally. Because she cannot combat the idea that novel-reading is dangerous, she seeks to have some works (hers among them) exempted from the general censure. Certainly those which "carry us too far from real life" must be read with extreme caution and only by those capable of separating "the truth from the fiction of the story." Truth (actuality) belongs on one side, fiction (possibility) on the other; grave danger results if the distinction between the two orders becomes blurred in any way.

A generic criticism of the novel based implicitly on the same metaphysics may also be found in Ann Eliza Bleecker's *The History of Maria Kittle*. The first letter of this epistolary novel begins, "However fond of novels and romances you may be, the unfortunate adventures of one of my neighbors who died yesterday, will make you despise that fiction, in which, knowing the subject to be fabulous, we can never be so truly interested."[19] And in *The Boarding School* (1798), Hannah Webster Foster warns that the images inspired by novels often warp one's notion of reality, perverting the judgment, misleading the affections, and blinding the understanding.[20] The results of such a melancholy series of events make up the theme of Mrs. Foster's *The Coquette* (1797), a novel very probably based on the tragic experiences and fatal seduction of Elizabeth Whitman of Hartford, which caused much contemporary comment.[21]

William Hill Brown alludes to the Elizabeth Whitman case in *The Power of Sympathy* and, in a footnote, gives a straightforward account of the details. Miss Whitman, of a reputable Connecticut family, was admired in her youth for beauty and good sense. But she was "a great reader of novels"; and from these "fallacious sources" she derived her idea of the character of men. After refusing several offers of marriage because they did not match up to her fanciful ideas, she became disappointed in "her *Fairy* hope" and ultimately engaged in an illicit romance. She became pregnant, a proposed husband deserted her, and she left her friends and travelled to Salem. "Here she wandered alone and friendless, and at length repaired to the *Bell-Tavern*, in *Danvers*, where she was delivered of a lifeless child, and in about a fortnight after [in July, 1788] died of a puerperal fever, aged about 35 years."[22] In the Boston *Independent Chronicle* of September 11, 1788, a writer directs attention to the moral lesson to be learned from these events; Miss Whitman, he remarks, was "a great reader of romances." A week later, a writer in the Boston *Massachusetts Centinel* placed the blame for the tragedy squarely on Miss Whitman's avid taste for fiction. She "formed her notions of happiness from that corrupt source," he says, "became vain and coquettish, and rejected some very advantageous offers of marriage in hope of realizing something more splendid. . . ."[23] Doubtless it was easy for moralistic critics of fiction to feel some sort of satisfaction at the principle involved in Miss Whitman's death. Here was proof of what they were saying; here was a girl who had (according to all reports) read fiction indiscriminately, who had permitted fiction to warp her sense of reality until she was no longer capable of coping with the actual world in a rational manner, until her impending doom could not be averted. Such a case history must have been worth dozens of bad novels to the critics of fiction. And for the novelist, who needed to have his fiction and damn it too, here was a body of fact worthy to ground his fiction upon.

In a sense, there had to be an Elizabeth Whitman; she symbolized what we might call a moral-fictional imperative, an object lesson for all to regard.

The pressures on the novel in early America thus work together into a complex of hostility. I have attempted to demonstrate that the crucial issue involved in the attack was one of metaphysics. Moreover, it seems to me that this metaphysics was not the private possession of a few men; the comments of critics who held differing views about the novel reveal a common metaphysical commitment; the critics assume that the public shares at least implicitly the same notions about reality—and they certainly seem to have been right. In short, there existed what we might call a metaphysical orthodoxy, the principles of which condemned the novel for metaphysical heterodoxy. It follows that a true defense of novels would have presupposed some sort of metaphysical revolution.

These critics of the novel were not, however, writing on metaphysical issues as such. Theirs is primarily moralistic criticism; its intention is to influence conduct, to persuade to the good, to dissuade from the evil. If we are to understand the appeal, function, and value of this criticism, we must see the most significant thing about it: its moralistic intent is sanctioned by metaphysics—the moral indictment of novels has metaphysical backing. Indeed, the metaphysical basis for adverse criticism of the novel is of such efficacy that even when a critic writes from outside the moralistic framework (as we have seen in the case of Joseph Dennie), his ideas conform to the principles of the orthodox metaphysics. Most often, however, moralistic criticism of fiction was allied to metaphysics, and the alliance of the two presented a case against the novel that was felt and acknowledged throughout the entire culture.

The Metaphysical Sanction

As would be expected, the most elaborate sections in the writings of the Scottish Common Sense philosophers are those relating to perception. Reid himself believed that his reputation as a philosopher derived from the manner in which he had refuted the "ideal theory"; Berkeley, he felt, had severed the bond between man and extramental reality; Hume had relentlessly advanced to a position of complete skepticism. Both had made ideas ("or images of things in the mind") the proper objects of thought, as Locke had done before them.[24] Always crediting Berkeley and especially Hume for providing a basis for his philosophical inquiry, Reid—and after him Dugald Stewart and Sir William Hamilton—sought to re-establish the validity of man's perception in terms of the primary, unimpeachable testimony of consciousness. What man saw and heard and felt was real, they contended; it was reality—concrete, external, extramental. This emphasis on the objective existence of extramental reality, so necessary for a rejection of idealistic thought, had, necessarily, a profound effect on the metaphysics of the Scottish realistic philosophers. It drove them to concentrate on the actually existing object, the perceivable entity; it begot a tendency to narrow the limits of reality to actually existing being. The order of possibility, it is true, was never denied, nor could it be; but possibles were conceived of in the mind—one could not perceive them in the same way. Hence, for one to conceive of possible being, to make a habit of so conceiving, was not altogether desirable, for dwelling on intramental existence might tempt one to succumb to the charms of a Berkeleian universe or resign himself to Humean skepticism. The whole movement of Scottish Common Sense metaphysics was out of the mind;

indeed, its total structure rests on the foundation of objectively, actually existing reality. The natural result of this emphasis is a metaphysics in which actuality holds the crucial and primary position.

As Thomas Reid and many persons since have noted, the principles of Common Sense philosophy are better suited to negate than to affirm, more fitted for refutation than for constructing a positive philosophical system. And in Reid's philosophical investigations there is little concern for building such an autonomous metaphysics. His is largely a philosophy of polite protest. Samuel Miller, among the Americans who saw Reid's thought in this light, wrote that although Reid "has taken much pains to overturn the old ideal system, he has not ventured to substitute any theory of his own in its place." To have attempted this, however, Miller continues, would have been inconsistent, for Reid's aim was "to give a simple and precise statement of facts, divested of all theoretical expressions; to show how long philosophers have imposed upon themselves by principles gratuitously assumed, and by words without meaning; and to convince them, that 'with respect to the process of nature in perception, they are no less ignorant than the vulgar.' " And let no one slight this, Miller says, "as a negative and unimportant discovery."[25]

Since the task of refutation calls for clarification and definition, however, Reid does set forth some metaphysical principles. He writes of "general conceptions," which may more properly be called "*compositions* or *works* than mere combinations" of previously conceived extramental objects. Thus, says Reid, "one may conceive a machine which never existed," or perhaps an "air in music, a poem, a plan in architecture, a plan of government, a plan of conduct in public or private life, a sentence, a discourse, a treatise." These compositions "are things conceived in the mind of the author, not individuals that really exist." Consequently, the author may communicate his general conception to others by language. But the works of God, according to Reid, are "very different" from these compositions, for "they are works of creative power, not of understanding only. They have a real existence." Reid concludes that our best conceptions of the works of God are only "partial and imperfect," while our conception of compositions of the human understanding may be "perfect and complete," because the latter are "nothing but what the author conceived, and what he can express by language, so as to convey his conception perfectly to men like himself."[26]

These statements of Reid contain the curious anomaly which runs deep in his metaphysics. The general conception of which he speaks "never existed"; they are "not individuals that really exist"; "they are nothing but what the author conceived." Thus, they are man-made, unreal things, existing in and through the action of the mind—*entia rationis*. The works of God, on the other hand, have a "real existence"; they are "very different." So we have set up an antithesis between man-created unreality and God-created reality analogous to the antithesis implicit in the criticism of the novel—and we note again that God is regarded as the only true creator. Reid clearly conceives of reality in terms of actuality: what is real is actual. But the anomalous, though logical, feature of Reid's discussion is his idea that man can know God's creation only partially and imperfectly, whereas he can know the unrealities conceived of by the mind completely and perfectly. The principle involved is that the finite mind cannot comprehend fully the creations, "works," of an infinite mind, whereas it can know perfectly and completely things conceived by another finite mind. But the implications of this position are enormous for a Scottish realist, for it was the inability to know extramental reality—

God's creation—that led philosophers to make ideas the proper objects of thought and to view reality as within the mind, a step which culminated in idealism, the very thing against which Reid and his followers reacted. Nowhere does Reid seem to see the potential precariousness of his position. The point, however, does bear indirectly on the question at hand and should be noted here: Reid distinguishes between two types of reality (or, in his terms, reality and unreality—to use the words loosely) and believes that the works of God—extramental reality—partake of a higher mode of existence than the imaginings of the human mind. His reference to God the creator as against man the creator, as well as his rhetorical treatment ("nothing but what the author conceives," etc.) of the works of these human creators testifies to his belief that actual reality is a better, a higher form of existence than are the things envisioned as possible by the human mind.[27]

The most concise and effective presentation of Scottish Common Sense metaphysics exists in the writings of Sir William Hamilton (1788–1856), who has been called "the ablest exponent and special defender of the Scottish realism."[28] Hamilton became Professor of Logic and Metaphysics at Edinburgh in 1836, after having been Professor of Universal History since 1821. The "most conspicuous figure" in nineteenth-century English philosophy, according to Noah Porter, Hamilton was "confessedly the most learned student of his time."[29] In 1861 Francis Bowen, then Alford Professor at Harvard, brought out an edition of *The Metaphysics of Sir William Hamilton*, "Collected, arranged and abridged for the use of colleges and private students"; Bowen felt that a course in mental philosophy which lacked "a tolerably full view" of Hamilton's metaphysics "must be very imperfect"; the importance of Hamilton's metaphysical principles seemed to him "likely to exert a considerable influence over English and American minds for many years to come."[30] Hamilton serves us here as a penetrating commentator, whose metaphysical analysis constitutes not a new pattern of thought but rather a detailed exposition of the metaphysics central to the spirit and tradition of Common Sense philosophy.

In his metaphysical inquiry, Hamilton distinguishes immediately between presentative and representative reality; he believes this primary distinction must be made by anyone in the tradition of Scottish realism. "A thing is known *immediately* or *proximately*," writes Hamilton in his edition of Reid's works, "when we cognize it *in itself; mediately or remotely* when we cognize it *in or through something numerically different from itself.*" Immediate cognition, by which Hamilton means the knowledge of "the thing in itself," involves the "*fact*" of the thing's existence; mediate cognition, that is, "the knowledge of a thing in or through something not itself, involves only the possibility" of the thing's existence.[31] Thus, an immediate cognition, a thing itself presented to observation, may be called presentative; a mediate cognition, a thing mirrored or held up to the mind in a vicarious representation, may be called representative.

Hamilton admits that the term "real" may be and has been made synonymous with actual, as opposed to potential or possible, existence. But he is careful to observe the distinction, which he sees as essential to his conception of realism. He delimits the orders of the actual and possible and defines—in relation to the human mind—the manner in which a being exists in each order. Of the actual order he writes,

a thing to be known *in itself* must be known as *actually existing*. . . and it cannot be known as actually existing unless it be known as existing in its *When* and its *Where*. But the When and Where of an object are immediately cognisable by the sub-

ject, only if the When be *now* (i. e. at the same moment with
the cognitive act,) and the Where be *here*, (i. e. within the
sphere of the cognitive faculty); therefore a presentative or
intuitive knowledge is only competent of an object present to
the mind, both in time and space.

Conversely, "whatever is known, but not as *actually* existing *now* and *here*, is not known in itself, as the presentative
object of an intuitive, but only as the remote object of a
representative, cognition." And the emphasis of Scottish
metaphysics on the actually existing, extramental object
becomes more evident in the light of Hamilton's treatment
of possibles. "A possible object," he continues, "an *ens
rationis*—is a mere fabrication of the mind itself." For Hamilton, it exists "only in and through an act of imagination, and
has only a logical existence, apart from that act with which
it is really identical. . . ." A possible object is thus "an intuitive object in itself," but only in that by not involving a
contradiction "it is conceived as prefiguring something
which may possibly exist some-where and some-when,—
this something, too, being constructed out of elements which
had been previously given in Presentation." It is, of course,
Representative.[32]

Even in defining these terms Hamilton evinces the metaphysical preference for actuality which pervades Scottish
realism. In these passages a rhetorical subordination of the
possible can be seen when Hamilton calls a possible object
a "mere" fabrication of the mind which has "only" a logical
existence. And in his conclusion, where he goes on to state
that the Natural Realists hold presentative cognition to be
"objective and absolute," and representative cognition, "under every form," to be "subjective and relative," the former
set of terms and not the latter is meant to demand respect
and approbation. Moreover, perhaps under the impact of

Berkeley and Hume (and Locke as well), Hamilton, along with Reid, tends to speak of possibles separately, singularly, discretely, as cognized individually, as beings of reason: both Hamilton and Reid are interested in being *as it relates to the human mind*. Reid's compositions are "things conceived in the mind of the author, not individuals that really exist"; Hamilton's possible object has a logical, not a real, existence. The remainder of his discussion sheds additional light on this tendency, highly significant for our purposes here.

Hamilton proceeds to a series of comparisons between actual and possible being which serve to emphasize distinctly the subordinate position of the order of possible reality. First he compares the two aspects of being "by reference to the *character of the existential Judgments* they involve":

the judgment involved in an Intuitive apprehension is *assertory;* for the fact of the intuition being dependent on the fact of the present existence of the object, the existence of the object is unconditionally enounced as actual.— The judgment involved in a Representative apprehension is problematic; for here the fact of the representation not being dependent on the present existence of the object represented, the existence of that object can be only modally affirmed as possible.

Again Hamilton is stressing the difference between actuality and possibility; something which exists only possibly is patently not existing as fully as a being which possesses actual existence. His next comparison is on the grounds of self-sufficiency: "Representative knowledge," he writes,

is *not self-sufficient,* in as much as every representative cognition of an object supposes a previous presentative apprehension of that same object. This is even true of the representation of an imaginary or merely possible object; for though the object, of which we are conscious in such an act, be a mere figment of the phantasy, and, as a now represented whole, was never previously presented to our observation; still that whole is nothing but an assemblage of parts, of which, in different combinations, we have had an intuitive cognition.—Presentative knowledge, on the contrary, is, in this respect, *self-sufficient*, being wholly independent of Representative for its objects.[33]

Furthermore, continues Hamilton, "Representative is dependent on Presentative knowledge, as (with the mind) the concause and condition of its possibility." But "Presentative knowledge is in this respect *independent* of Representative; for with our intuitive cognitions, commences all our knowledge." A representative cognition, a cognition derived from the realm of possibility, is thus taken to be inferior because of the inferior quality of the very order of possible being; this order is dependent, insufficient to exist of itself.

In his final comparison, Hamilton makes this point unequivocally. "Intuitive knowledge," he states, "is *complete* and *perfect*"; it affords "the highest certainty of the highest determination of existence—the Actual—the Here and Now existent." But representative knowledge, "*incomplete* and *imperfect*," affords "only an inferior assurance of certain inferior determinations of existence—the Past, the Future, the Possible—the not Here and not Now existent."[34] Though Hamilton may be technical, he is always explicit. His detailed analysis and exposition of a metaphysics which evolved out of a quest for valid and sure knowledge have one emphatic meaning: because of its extreme emphasis on the validity of the actually existing object, Scottish realism gives a position of metaphysical superiority to the actual order and thus to actually existing being. The order of possibility is subordinate, dependent, inferior, incomplete, imperfect, insufficient of itself, whereas the order of actuality is the antithesis of all of these things—it affords "the highest certainty of the highest determination of existence." The word "certainty" suggests matters epistemological, and, in a very important sense, it was the desire to construct a valid and defensible epistemology that led the Scottish realists to make such an extreme metaphysical commitment to the actual order.

Hamilton's discussion, analogous in structure and metaphysical preference to the work of Reid and Stewart, allows us to see what the Scottish realists were consistently endeavoring to prove. The burden of Common Sense metaphysics is to establish the existence of extramental reality, of a reality outside and independent of the mind.

I have no wish to enter here upon a consideration of essence and existence, one of the liveliest issues of our contemporary philosophical inquiry; I should like merely to suggest that one step the Scots might have taken to arrive at their desiderated position would have been to posit a throughgoing ontological realism—an order of possibility as well as an order of actuality outside and independent of the mind. But they did not take this step. And if one contends that it is implicit in their approach, the only answer is that they did not seem to realize it, gave no explicit attention to it, placed no emphasis on it. For their emphasis was placed in another quarter.

Let us not forget that Reid began negatively, admitting his large debt to Berkeley and Hume. This is the initial significant fact we must keep in mind. For in attempting to demonstrate that Berkeley and Hume were incorrect, Reid did not turn away and work toward a complete positive system. He altered, in the name of common sense; he modified at crucial places, following, as it were, some law of intellectual parsimony. He thought not of a complete order of being outside the mind, but of individual extramental objects; or, to make the matter clear by stating it in the extreme, he broke out of the mind by finding one thing out-side at a time. His method of discussion came thus to center on material, individual objects. These objects were to him the best, most available evidence of the existence of extra-mental reality; they were also his common-sense evidence.

All of the later Scottish realists, though they amended and completed Reid and seldom agreed with him entirely, in-herited from him both the negative response to Berkeley and Hume and the method of proving the existence of the extramental world by referring to individual objects in it. The result of such a reaction and such a method was two-fold: first, no explicit attention was given to an objectively existing order of possibility—the question simply did not present itself in these terms; second, when possibles were spoken of, as they must be in some way in any metaphysical system, they were spoken of as individual possible objects; and they were located in the mind, since, as Hamilton says, they are mere fabrications of the mind, existing only ideally in and through an act of imagination, having only a logical existence. For Hamilton, a possible object is an *ens rationis*. In the light of what the Scottish realists were reacting against, their metaphysical preference for the actually exist-ing object over that existing possibly (in the mind) follows as a matter of course.

Hamilton's inquiries evidence a metaphysics analogous to that implicit in the criticism of fiction in America. Both view being in a dual aspect, as actual and as possible; both believe actual being to be of a higher, more complete, and "safer" order than possible being, which has existence only in and through an act of the mind. Indeed, Hamilton's own definition of *entia rationis* suggests another term—beings of imagination—which, I think, at once classifies in its own right and describes what happened to the concepts and cate-gories of Scottish metaphysics when they were brought to

bear on fiction in America, a change conditioned by a different if finally related object of inquiry. But the analogy
between Scottish realism and American criticism of fiction
is not yet in full view. The ideas of Dugald Stewart, particularly on being as conceived imaginatively, shed additional light on the analogy and on the relationship of the
actual and possible.

Stewart distinguishes between conception and imagination: "the province of the former," he writes, "is to present
us with an exact transcript of what we have formerly felt
and perceived; that of the latter, to make a selection of
qualities and of circumstances from a variety of different
objects, and by combining and disposing these, to form a
new creation of its own."[35] Conception, then, equates with
memory; one may, indeed should, cultivate it fearlessly. But
imagination, a faculty which can create reality to its own
taste, is dangerous and must be used with caution. In another
place Stewart defines imagination as "a faculty which is
habitually conversant with creations of its own, more perfect than what the world presents to us."[36] And again he
writes that cultivating the imagination does not diminish
one's interest in human life, but is "extremely apt to inspire
the mind with false conceptions" of life. The chief gratification of the imagination lies in its tendency to picture "to
itself" things more perfect than those which exist; consequently, it has another tendency, to "exalt our expectations
above the level of our present conditions." Frequently, says
Stewart, the imagination "produces a youth of enthusiastic
hope, while it stores up disappointment and disgust for our
maturer years."[37]

The warnings of Stewart about the function of the imagination and the fulminations of American critics on the subject are essentially the same. Moreover, both are motivated
by the idea that possibles, existing (ideally) in the mind,

constitute an inferior order of being. For the American critic, possible being was dangerous because in the distorted notion of reality it yielded one could not discover truth. Stewart agrees; but the case of the Scottish realists against possible reality is much stronger and, moreover, metaphysically explicit. As Hamilton demonstrated, possible reality is dependent, inferior, and imperfect; it is a subordinate type of being, subordinate to actuality. And yet, through the workings of the imagination one may utilize this metaphysically inferior aspect of reality and construct possible beings which appear more perfect than those which exist actually. These possible beings are monsters because they are constructs patched together from one's experience with actuality. They are, in fact, one's own creations, and to become accustomed to them, or to get to like them, is to run the risk of becoming dissatisfied with actual reality—God's creation. Stewart is aware of the danger of misplacing one's metaphysical emphasis, of coming to prefer the apparently better but metaphysically inferior things of the imagination to actuality. "It was undoubtedly the intention of Nature," he writes, "that the objects of perception should produce much stronger impressions on the mind than its own operations." Proper training early in life gives assurance that such will be the case. But it is possible to reverse the "order of things," to acquire a preference for the inner and artificial rather than the outer and real world. "Long habits of solitary reflection," for example, may cause us to lose touch with "sensible objects" to such an extent that our conduct will come "almost wholly under the influence of imagination." Apart from society, withdrawn from the pursuits of life, habituated to the contemplation of our own thoughts, "we are apt to contract an unnatural predilection for meditation, and to lose all interest in external occurrences." The "bustle of the world," corrective and sanative if at times annoying, no longer commands our attention. And in such a situation, concludes Stewart, "the mind gradually loses that command which education, when properly conducted, gives it over the train of its ideas; till at length the most extravagant dreams of imagination acquire as powerful an influence in exciting all its passions, as if they were realities."[38]

That Stewart, in telling us how one loses touch with reality, places the initial blame on the intellect is not surprising. Apart from intercourse with everyday reality, he feels, the intellect is a prey to the fallacies of idealism. The Scottish realists uniformly insist that the mind must keep in touch with objective reality; the actual order not only partakes of the highest order of finite existence, is not only the foundation of knowledge, but works as a constant corrective to the idealistic tendencies of the intellect. With the intellect weakened by divorce from actuality, the working of the imagination may bring about a complete dislocation of the mind from reality. The strong theme of anti-intellectualism evident in this passage finds an analogue in the advice of Dr. James Gray to study human nature "in the drawing room, not in the library, in the forum, not in the cloister." And there is likewise a similarity of tone in Gray's advice on novel-reading and Stewart's comments on the dangers of an ill-regulated imagination. Each states his case cautiously, carefully, but in such a way that disagreement will be out of the question for any right-thinking man.

On the dangers of "an excessive indulgence in the pleasures of imagination" Stewart adds a final warning, which is especially pertinent here because of its specific attention to novel-reading. The passage could well have come from one of the American critics of fiction. By overusing the imagination, says Stewart, we may refine our tastes to a point of fastidiousness wholly unsuitable to the "present situation of human nature." We may neglect to form our intellectual and moral habits by actual experience with the world and gradually accommodate them to the "dreams of poetry and romance." Not only will habits so formed "disqualify" us from performing the duties belonging by right to our station in life; a mind given over to imaginative excess is in "a distempered state." It is an "endless source of error," particularly at those critical times when our decisions determine future happiness or misery, when most of all we require the judgment to be calm and objective, formed by proper habits. Unfortunately, fiction tends to focus on such critical situations, exploiting them because of their inherent (but dangerous) interest. "The effect of novels, in misleading the passions of youth, with respect to the most interesting and most important of relations, is one of the many instances of the inconveniences resulting from an ill-regulated imagination."[39] Turning his attention directly to "fictitious compositions," Stewart advances his most fundamental reasons for mistrusting the imagination as one sees it in fiction. Again it seems to me important to quote in full; only by seeing the original form of the argument can one appreciate Stewart's attitude toward fiction and, more importantly, his grounds for that attitude. "It will not, I think, be disputed," he begins,

that the frequent perusal of pathetic compositions diminishes the uneasiness which they are naturally fitted to excite. A person, who indulges habitually in such studies, may feel a growing desire of his usual gratifications, but he is every day less and less affected by the scenes which are presented to him. I believe it would be difficult to find an actor long hackneyed on the stage, who is capable of being completely interested by the distresses of a tragedy. The effect of such compositions and representations, in rendering the mind callous to actual distress, is still greater; for as the imagination of the Poet almost always carries him beyond truth and nature, a familiarity with the tragic scenes, which he exhibits, can hardly fail to deaden the impression produced by the comparatively trifling sufferings which the ordinary course of human affairs presents to us. In real life, a provision is made for this gradual decay of sensibility, by the proportional decay of other passive impressions, which have an opposite tendency, and by the additional force which our active habits are daily acquiring. Exhibitions of fictitious distress, while they produce the former change on the character, have no influence in producing the latter; on the contrary, they tend to strengthen these passive impressions which counteract beneficence. The scenes into which the Novelist introduces us are, in general, perfectly unlike those which occur in the world. As his object is to please, he removes from his descriptions every circumstance which is disgusting, and presents us with histories of elegant and dignified distress. It is not such scenes that human life exhibits. We have to act, not with refined and elegant characters, but with the mean, the illiterate, the vulgar, and the profligate. The perusal of fictitious history has a tendency to increase that disgust, which we naturally feel at the concomitants of distress, and to cultivate a false refinement of taste, inconsistent with our condition as members of society. Nay it is possible for this refinement to be carried so far, as to withdraw a man from the duties of life, and even from the sight of those distresses which he might alleviate. And, accordingly, many are to be found, who, if the situation of romances were realized, would not fail to display the virtues of their favorite characters, whose sense of duty is not sufficiently strong to engage them in the humble and private scenes of human misery.

To these effects of fictitious history we may add, that it gives no exercise to our active habits. In real life we proceed from the passive impression to those exertions which it was intended to produce. In the contemplation of imaginary sufferings, we stop short at the impression, and whatever benevolent dispositions we may feel, we have no opportunity of carrying them into action.

"From these reasonings," concludes Stewart, "it appears that an habitual attention to exhibitions of fictitious distress, is in every view calculated to check our moral improvement." He does not "disapprove entirely of fictitious narratives"; on the contrary, he believes "that the perusal of them may be attended with advantage, when the efforts I have mentioned are corrected by the habits of real business." He means "to insinuate" that a taste for fiction "may be carried too far; that the sensibility which terminates in imagination, is but a refined and selfish luxury; and that nothing can effectually advance our moral improvement, but an attention to the active duties which belong to our stations."[40]

Because of the basic distinction between actuality and possibility inherent in his writings and central to the Common Sense conception of reality, Stewart cannot regard fictitious or possible experience as something which can be transferred to or assimilated by actual experience. Fiction is a stimulant created by the imagination of man: the reader perceives in fiction scenes of distress, of pathos, of tragedy; naturally these scenes stimulate a desire to act; but there can be no action, no alleviation; the situation is static, set. And gradually, as one is exposed to more and more of these scenes, he becomes inured. When he turns to the life of actuality, the life he must live, when he confronts similar scenes, only less perfect because dynamic and actual, the same hardening of stimulus-response patterns will be in effect, and his actions will be less beneficent, less charitable, less moral than they should be. The better-than-life images created by the imagination are therefore extremely dangerous to one's moral well-being and ultimately to the moral fibre of society. In the words of Dr. James Gray, "they can do no good," since "that extravagance of vice which does not occur in real life can never answer the purpose of deterring us from vitious indulgence; and virtues which have never

been practised can scarcely become examples." Gray likewise refers to novels as "a species of artificial stimulant," as
"chamber cordials." And, indeed, in terms of the metaphysics from which the ideas of Stewart and Gray are derived,
the novel—and fiction—could be regarded as nothing else. As
a stimulant, it could also act as a drug, so it became necessary
for someone to warn against the danger of addiction. This
was the function of the critic, who spoke to and for an
already convinced society about the grave peril of indulging
the imagination.

Confirmation

In his *Dissertations Moral and Critical* (1783) James Beattie
expresses from a slightly different point of view the ideas
common to Scottish realists on this subject. Like Stewart,
Beattie distinguishes between memory and imagination: in
remembering, he says, "we revolve or revise past perceptions, with a view to our experience of them, and to their
reality"; in imagining, however, "we consider the notion or
thought now present in the mind, simply as it is in itself,
without any view to real existence, or to past experience."
From the imagination we get ideas "without any view to
their reality."[41] Once again, in the distinction between what
is real and what is not real, we see the imagination as a
faculty of unreality, out of space, time, and experience,
working in a kind of vacuum. Although he is not dealing
with metaphysical inquiry as such, Beattie's distinction
between memory and imagination rests securely on the
Scottish metaphysics. In view of this distinction (and its
metaphysical basis), Beattie's warning against fiction follows
logically. It is a "dangerous recreation"; it "breeds a dislike
for history, and all the substantial parts of knowledge; with-
draws the attention from nature and truth; and fills the mind

with extravagant thoughts, and too often with criminal propensities."[42] Wedded to memory, history constantly introduces what is real; wedded to imagination, fiction constantly introduces what is not real. Since no synthesis is possible in these terms, one must either withdraw his attention "from nature and truth" or resist the siren song of the imagination, for, again, the indulgence of the imagination is fraught with peril.

Thomas Brown, speaking of the human desire for knowledge, explains that our minds seek out everything which we are capable of knowing, not "realities merely," but also "the extravagance of fiction." He sees all fiction as at bottom a variation of the "tales of our nursery"; in our later, or "graver," years we call these tales romances, dramas, and epics, but we are always ready in moments of leisure "to be led away by any narrative of strange incidents." Unfortunately, however, fiction frequently stimulates without satisfying our curiosity: tales are often "intentionally suspended at some most interesting moment, and printed as fragments." In such cases, says Brown, we feel pain and a vexation amounting almost to anger, as if the author were "wilfully and wantonly" inflicting injury upon us. Fiction to Brown is not only the extravagance of the real, but a potential instrument of masochism: "To be forced to read a succession of such fragments would be truly to any mind which can take interest in the adventures of others, a species of torture, and of torture that, to such a mind, would be far from being the slightest which could be devised."[43] And, since one's decision to read fiction is, in practical fact, voluntary, self-torture must be added to self-delusion as part of the case against fiction.

One further aspect of Scottish thought, important here because its concern with esthetics and criticism gave it a direct and easily discernible bearing on the principles of

American criticism, may serve to complete our examination of the conceptual basis afforded the American critic by Common Sense philosophy. As we know, American criticism was primarily moralistic, in tone as well as intent; the significant point is that this moralistic criticism had metaphysical sanction. Perhaps the American critic—clergyman, educator, lawyer—shared in the Puritan tendency to view all actions in terms of ultimate significance—good or bad, right or wrong, heaven or hell. At any rate, the moralistic element in his work was all-pervasive: questions of criticism, metaphysics, or epistemology were not separate from those of morality. The critic saw the world and the questions in the world as a unity—a moral unity.

In the same manner Scottish Common Sense philosophy regarded matters of knowledge, of being, of criticism, of morality, as one. A critical or metaphysical misstep would have a moral consequence. The work of Lord Kames shows us particularly the alliance of morality and criticism—an alliance which American critics assumed as natural. "A taste in the fine arts," writes Kames, "goes hand in hand with the moral sense, to which indeed it is nearly allied. Both of them discover what is right and what is wrong. . . . Neither of them are arbitrary or local. They are rooted in human nature, and are governed by principles common to all men."[44] Again, Kames writes that the most important advantage of criticism lies in its "great support to morality."[45] Any American critic would agree wholeheartedly with Kames. The Scottish conception of the function of criticism marks a final analogy between the explicit philosophical formulations of Common Sense realism and the implicit philosophical position of the American critic of fiction. Scottish realism said and proved what the American critic assumed.

3

THE WORLD WITHOUT AND THE
WORLD WITHIN: FICTION AND
THE AMERICAN IMAGINATION

Chapter Three

THE LOGICAL precision of the case against fiction, involved as it was with the desire for social and moral stability, had a profound effect on the American imagination. From such men as James Gray and Samuel Miller, Americans heard what they wanted to hear—that there were dangers inherent in novel reading, that fiction bred false conceptions of life, unhappiness, dissatisfaction with everyday existence, perhaps even criminal tendencies. The result, itself implicit in the cause, was a fear of imaginative experience. The order of possibility, in which the imagination had perforce to work, could do nothing but challenge the stability and safety of society; if the processes of history, under the guiding hand of God, had made America what it was, any sort of commitment to fiction and the imagination could seem only an act of folly. The world of the imagination thus became in a special way a region of terror. Granted that men always and everywhere have been able to inspire terror via the imagination; in the United States, with the imagination regarded as a threat to society, the terror took on a new and local dimension.

In his *Inaugural Address* in 1817 Levi Frisbie warned of the "magick of fiction and poetry," the implication of course being that magic is dangerous.[1] And we may recall Emerson's statement that Reid's ideas, helpful as they were, had not completely removed the "terror which attached to the name of Hume." Philosophy, political theory, fiction, indeed, any human endeavor might constitute a threat to American well-being and inspire a kind of terror. But Americans did not have to sit passively and endure such terror. Common Sense thought was a way of combating it; if it could not be eliminated, at least it could be controlled. The "terror" of Hume could be put at a distance and made almost irrelevant by the enlightened sanity of Reid and Stewart; the terror of fiction could be neutralized by the Scottish metaphysic and effectively reduced by history. Means there were, then, to keep the imagination in its place; and when the imagination operated, when, that is, an investigation into the order of possibility occurred, as it would and did despite all, the means of control would have significant effects on the achieved imaginative product.

Imagination, Realism, and Instinct

Since Americans thought about the imagination largely in terms supplied by the Scots, it will be well briefly to place in perspective the concept of imagination held generally by the Common Sense school. Two complementary points must be kept in mind: that the Scottish idea of the imagination was primarily mechanistic; and, as we have seen in Chapter Two, that the beings invented by the imagination were taken to be unreal and hence metaphysically inferior to actual being.

Dugald Stewart, we recall, distinguished between conception (memory) and imagination and granted the imagination the function of combining elements of former experience into new assemblages of its own. James Beattie makes essentially the same distinction—in his terms, between remembrance and imagination—and leaves no doubt as to which is the higher, preferred faculty. It is possible for us to imagine a thing, Beattie says, without being able to refer it in any way to our experience; at times, however, when one is imagining something in this manner, he is suddenly able to locate the thing in his experience. At such a moment imagination becomes remembrance (fiction becomes history), and one has a feeling of satisfaction explained by the fact that he has restored a higher kind of reality to the thing.[2] Beattie gives the imagination the dual power of "apprehending or conceiving ideas, simply as they are in themselves, without any view to their reality," and of "combining into new forms, or assemblages, those thoughts, ideas, or notions, which we have derived from experience, or from information."[3] Both Stewart and Beattie insist on the metaphysical inferiority of the new assemblages; they are mere constructs, mechanically put together, which have never had actual existence.

Thomas Reid's "general conceptions" or compositions differ from the ordinary constructs of Beattie and Stewart and seem to put us closer to a dynamic, organic idea of the imagination. To present the conception of a poem or a piece of music or an architectural plan as distinct from the combination of assemblages appears to be reaching beyond mechanistic explanations of the imagination. But Reid undercuts the existential quality of these compositions (and thus the validity of the imaginative function) by means of the inexorable Scottish metaphysic: since these compositions exist only in the minds of men, they lack the perfection and reality of actual being. In short, the Scottish metaphysic dictated a response to imaginatively considered being; allied with the mechanist tradition, it made and could make no provision for synthesis or "creation" and was not prepared to validate the constructs of the imagination.

In perpetuating the alliance of Common Sense metaphysics and the mechanist theory of imagination, Lord Kames, along with Beattie, Stewart, and Archibald Alison, stressed that the imagination calls up images in terms of all one's associated experience. The Scottish writers, as Martin Kallich points out, were developing a notion of association that had been formulated earlier by Hobbes, who regarded the association of ideas as a natural phenomenon of the mind as well as the best explanation of the coherence of our expression and thought.[4] Consistently emphasizing neoclassical rules of criticism and standards of taste, the Scots employed association psychology to illuminate the workings of the imagination. As part of the mechanist conception of the imagination, it served them well, resolving the processes of literary invention in a manner that could readily be appreciated and understood, characterizing the imagination as an orderly, predictable, and hence reliable faculty. But the road of mechanism and associationism was the very road travelled by Coleridge, who finally rebelled against what he felt were the fundamental limitations of the whole concept in an attempt adequately to explain the process of artistic creation. In his well known distinction between imagination and fancy, Coleridge categorizes the Scottish (and mechanist) concept of the imagination as fancy—distinctly the lesser faculty. "The Fancy," says Coleridge, almost exactly duplicating James Beattie's definition of the imagination, "is indeed no other than a mode of Memory emancipated from the order of time and space." Like memory, "the Fancy must receive all its materials ready made from the law of association." The imagination for Coleridge may be either primary or secondary. He defines the primary imagination as "the living Power and prime Agent of all Human Perception, and as a repetition in the finite mind of the eternal act of creation in the infinite I am." Although both elements of the definition are of great significance and cannot finally be separated, the final one is I believe crucial here: by means of the primary imagination the finite mind shares in the eternal act of creation, repeating and hence partaking of the creativity of pure, infinite existence. Coleridge sets up no opposition between God as creator and man as creator; in the highest sense there is only one act of creation, which man to his glory may share by means of the primary imagination. The secondary imagination is "an echo" of the primary, "co-existing with the conscious will," identical with the primary "in the kind of its agency," differing only "in degree" and in "the mode of its operation." "It dissolves, diffuses, dissipates, in order to re-create; or where this process is rendered impossible, yet still at all events it struggles to idealize and to unify." The unmistakable difference between the Scottish concept of the imagination and that of Coleridge can be seen again in his final statement regarding the secondary imagination: "It is essentially *vital*, even as all objects (as objects) are essentially fixed and dead."[5] Vital, living, and dynamic, Coleridge's idea of the imagination stands apart from the mechanist, static conception of the Scots (which deals with objects as objects) as quite something new. There is no way to account for it in the terms of Common Sense metaphysics, for it represents a new approach to reality—autonomous and creative.[6]

The term "creation," as M. H. Abrams indicates, had been worn into a routine critical term even in the early nineteenth century. In the philosophy and criticism of Coleridge, however, it took on new life as it imparted a fundamental vitality "to the existing analogy between the poet and the creative God."[7] Such an analogy, audacious, historically tempting, and capable of being viewed as near blasphemy, was, as we have seen, precisely what drew the fire of the moralist-critic. We recall the refrain: the artist plays at being God; the artist usurps the role of God; but since he is fallible and finite, he can only fail in his attempt to create; and our job is to preserve ourselves from involvement in his failure. The whole notion of artistic *creation* (traditionally involving the poet) would pose a religious and metaphysical threat to the critic schooled in Common Sense thought, for whom God was creative and man was inventive, with the imagination locked inside a reality which it did not create and was constrained to use according to certain principles.

Much has been said, quite erroneously I believe, about the innatism implicit in Thomas Reid's use of such terms as instinct and intuition. Alexander Everett, we recall, charged that the principles of Scottish realism led one to the notion of innate ideas, which the Scots have not "developed and proved as such." And such a contention became a commonplace criticism of the principles of Common Sense thought. If the criticism is valid, and if innatism is taken to imply idealism, Reid's metaphysics could conceivably be read as notes toward a Coleridgean, or any other idealistic, metaphysics—and not very well written notes at that. It is thus important to see that such criticism is misleading and incorrect; misinterpreting Reid's key terms, it fails to comprehend the quality of his realism. Reid's terminology does indeed invite and breed confusion; James Mackintosh observed in 1835 that philosophers risk trouble when they "borrow vague and inappropriate terms" from ordinary usage. And no man, says Mackintosh, affords a more striking instance of this danger than Reid, with "his two most unfortunate terms, *Common Sense* and *Instinct*." Not even a man searching for improper words "could have discovered any more unfit than these two"; for Reid meant to denote the law, state, or faculty of mind by which we immediately acknowledge certain simple truths as "the foundation of all reasoning" and "the necessary ground of all belief."[8]

Reid was aware of the potential source of confusion and error in his use of the word *sense*, which meant one thing in common language and another in the idiom of philosophical discussion. Philosophers, he says, have largely used this word without including any notion of judgment in its definition: they have divorced, verbally, sense and judgment. But in common language "sense always implies judgement": a man of good sense is considered to be a man of good judgment— and "nonsense is what is evidently contrary to right judgement." The most common meaning becomes for Reid the most proper meaning. Appropriating this ordinary or common meaning of the word *sense*, which he believes has the authority of etymology, history, and contemporary usage behind it, he defines common sense as "that degree of judgement which is common to men with whom we can converse and transact business."[9] (We may thus see how the criticism of men who were influenced by Reid and the Scottish realists would be eminently a "judicial" criticism, in William Charvat's term.) The province of common sense is "to judge of things self-evident." No rules, no discipline, no practice can supply this common sense, for it is an internal sense, an "inward light. . . given by heaven to different persons in different degrees." Again, Reid calls it a "gift of heaven," and, yet again, "a pure gift of heaven."[10]

Even before Reid struggled to formulate his idea of common sense, Lord Kames had explained what was for him our intuitive knowledge of the world in terms of internal senses or faculties. Yet intuitive knowledge comes through the external senses—modes of direct, immediate perception which must be believed: "That the objects of our external senses really exist in the way and manner we perceive," says Kames, "is a branch of intuitive knowledge."[11] Such a dictum, of course, is a recognizable anticipation of Reid's theory of the direct perception of external reality, one of the axioms of the Scottish school. Sir William Hamilton echoes Kames and Reid when he says (as we may recall from his exposition of Scottish metaphysics) that "with our intuitive cognitions, commences all our knowledge." And in using the word intuitive, these men are all referring to man's direct, immediate apprehension of the *external* world.

The use of such terms as intuition, instinctive, and common (internal) sense, all capable of a meaning widely different from that intended by Reid and the Scots, allowed Common Sense thought to be reasoned to conclusions unforeseen by its originators. It might seem that the Scottish realists wanted to subvert their realism and have it too. But any student of Common Sense philosophy who extends its principles to an idealist position has run the wrong way with the ball; we may understand perfectly how he got there, but he has nonetheless gone the wrong way. Reid's true position, I believe, is exemplified by a statement of Charles Sanders Peirce, who makes short work of any quibbles over the matter of instinctive powers. Every animal must have habits, says Peirce; "consequently, it must have *in posse* innate cognitive habits, which is all that anybody but John Locke ever meant by innate ideas. To say that I hold this for true is implied in my confession of the doctrine of Common-Sense—not quite that of the old Scotch School, but a critical philosophy of common sense."[12] For Peirce, '*in posse* innate cognitive habits" are simply built-in ways of knowing the outside world as the outside world.

Though Reid's phraseology is unfortunately not so terse or so vigorously precise as that of Peirce, his epigraphs to *An Inquiry into the Human Mind on the Principles of Common Sense* and to *Essays on the Intellectual Powers of Man*, both from the Book of Job, are I think pertinent here in leading us to the same conclusion: the first, "The inspiration of the Almighty giveth them understanding"; the second, "Who hath put wisdom in the inward parts?" Man contains his wisdom, man possesses within himself his capacity for valid judgment. But these are gifts, "pure gift[s] of heaven," given to man by God, the unique Creator of the universe. By means of these gifts man is able to live an intelligent, empirical existence, in touch with and in the context of the world outside himself. They are the means to a valid empiricism; refusal to accept them as axiomatic (and here is the crux of the matter) forces man back to self-formulated modes of perceiving the external world and to humanly invented categories for knowing. Just as God is the author of history and man the author of fiction, so God has given us internal senses with which to judge, while philosophers have given us merely obfuscating verbal formulations. In this light, God inspires Job to understanding because the irrefragable reality of Job's experience threatens to break him down. With "wisdom in the inward parts," however, Job is empowered with right judgment (though it may always be difficult to think of Job as a man of common sense). Such, I take it, is the tenor of Reid's argument, defining his intended position. The argument may be circular and verbally imprecise; but Reid was a realist unafraid of instincts, who, indeed, thought that a valid realism must incorporate instinctive and internal knowledge as a part of its own method of apprehending reality.

Transcendence *vs.* the Culture of the Imagination

The quest for a freer, more dynamic concept of the imagination was to occur in America as well as abroad. In criticism Charles Astor Bristed's preference for Hazlitt, Coleridge, and Carlyle, with their "wild strokes of nature," rather than the "canons and categories" of Campbell and Kames signalled a growing dissatisfaction with the limitations of the Scottish esthetic. In 1829, James Marsh had written a lengthy "Preliminary Address" to his edition of Coleridge's *Aids to Reflection,* in which he discussed the deficiencies of empiricism and common sense and the deep religious profit to be gained from studying Coleridge. Marsh stressed the importance of exploring and unfolding the "deeper and more solemn mysteries of our being"; each man must discover for himself "truths of vast discernment" which live "at a great depth."[13] Unfortunately, however, empiricism and common sense, the "prevailing system of metaphysics" in America, have failed to provide such knowledge. In words that well describe the central position held by the writings of Locke and the Scots in America, Marsh laments the dominance they have acquired:

It is our peculiar misfortune in this country, that while the philosophy of Locke and the Scottish writers has been received in full faith, as the only rational system, and its leading principles especially passed off as unquestionable, the strong attachment to religion, and the fondness for speculation, by both of which we are strongly characterized, have led us to combine and associate these principles, such as they are, with our religious interests and opinions, so variously and so intimately, that by most persons they are considered as necessary parts of the same system; and from being so long contemplated together, the rejection of one seems impossible without doing violence to the other.

Marsh wonders if men can "stand in doubt of this Philosophy *altogether*" without risking the "charge of heresy in Religion."[14]

Marsh's interest in Coleridge was fundamentally religious; his transcendentalism is conservative, best read, in the words of Lewis S. Feuer, as "a neo-Calvinism with an insistence on human evil."[15] But with the transcendentalism of the avid socialistic thinkers, or that of Emerson and Thoreau, it had one obvious and basic element in common: it located the highest truth and reality within. Marsh would emphasize the profound truths lying deep within us; Emerson would regard every natural fact as symbolic of a spiritual fact; Thoreau would tell us to explore whole continents within us. Not at all denying the existence of the external world, these men would assert the reality of a vastly more important inner truth. (It is this tendency not only to know and trust, but to explore oneself that led Henry James to say that in this respect New England introspection played almost the part of a social resource.) Thus it is not surprising that Thomas Reid with his intuitions and epigraphs from Job could push an Emerson or a Thoreau toward idealism. What should be remarked is the residual ambiguity of the Scottish terminology that would lead Marsh to lament the centrality of Common Sense thought, while Emerson could use the same doctrine for his own purposes. For Marsh it was an obstacle to knowing the inner man; to Emerson it was a stepping stone.[16]

Thus as a reaction to Common Sense concepts and also because of them, a view of the imagination as a creative, dynamic, and organic force began to take form from the 1830's onward, even while the principles of Scottish realism were dominant in the colleges and throughout the society. Transcendental thought, discrete and unharmonious, forming no organized system, marked an idealistic breaking away from the Scottish mode of viewing and classifying reality. "There are to most men moments when the actual becomes transparent, and reveals to their view the rich and magnificent world of the Ideal lying beyond, its basis and its possibility. To all intense and energetic action the Actual becomes merely a symbol of the Ideal."[17] The author of these words is Orestes Brownson, though they could well

have been written by any of a number of men; the statement exemplifies a general impetus to push beyond the limits
of realism and empiricism to a position from which one
might see the ideal as the "basis" and "possibility" of the
actual. Such a step, of course, had large implications for
one's concept of the imagination. And in Brownson's analysis of the imagination we may see how completely a different metaphysical emphasis altered the terms and problems
of the discussion.

For Brownson, the operation of the imagination involves
both reason and perception; in marked contrast to Beattie,
Brownson believes that the imagination perceives "in time
as well as in space." Although the literal meaning of the
word implies the representation of images to the mind, perhaps images of actual existences, the operation of the imagination is "chiefly concerned with *ideal* existences"; moreover, "its essence consists rather in the degree of intenseness
and energy with which those existences are perceived, than
in the mode in which they are expressed or represented."[18]
This immediate insistence on intensity and energy signifies
an emphasis on the vitality rather than the formality of the
imagined object, an emphasis that is common to most transcendentalist thinkers; *intenseness* and *energy* become for
Brownson the key factors in imaginative perception, suggesting direct, highly personal, in effect anti-formal contact
between the imaginer and the thing imagined. Perhaps implicit in Brownson's definition of the essence of the imagination is a tendency to value the discrete facts of reality
according to the intensity of subjective experience. But
Brownson explicitly shies away from equating the ideal and
the subjective; he contends strongly for the objectivity of
the ideal order. In an act of imagination, he says, there are
both subject and object; because the object is primarily
ideal, it is often held to be "a mode, affection, or creation of
the subject," and thus "wholly subjective and without ob-

jective validity." Hence, he continues, imaginary comes to mean fictitious, unreal, without solid foundation.[19] But Brownson takes issue with such a view: he considers the object in an act of imagination as a "not me," a thing existing independently of the subject or imaginer, not, thus, a being of reason (or of imagination), but a being having real existence.

For Brownson, all human activity is creative. For some philosophers, however, imagination is *the* creative faculty because it affords the highest degree of activity of which man is capable. By means of imagination a man operates at his creative best, enabled by the possession of a superior degree of sensibility to see life more intensely and energetically than most men; the expression of this heightened perception will require the "vivid and expressive" language of the imagination, the idiom of poetry.[20] In this context the term creation comes to mean discovery, for to Brownson the true act of imagination consists of perceiving the ideal in, or underlying, the actual (the ideal, we recall, exists for Brownson as the basis and possibility of the actual). Some persons "rarely if ever get through the Actual"; the poet, the artist, the man capable of energetic and intense perception, however, gets "through" because of his sensibility. "Poetry consists in the intense and energetic detection and representation of the Ideal in the Actual." The poet does not make the ideal, but finds it—"as truly objective as the Actual in which he finds it." For the ideal exists "out of us, and independent of us; only it exists as the Ideal, not as the Actual." Indeed, the actual exists only by virtue of the ideal. Thus, although he realizes that this is not the common opinion, Brownson concludes that the imagination, "by dealing with the Ideal, no more deals with the unsubstantial, the fictitious, the suppositious, the chimerical, or the subjective, than though it dealt solely with the Actual."[21]

But what about monsters, fairies, demons, and the like?

Brownson asks. Do they exist objectively and independently? He answers that like every object of the imagination
such beings are not-me; consequently they have an objective,
ideal existence—they exist as facts of memory; they belong
not to the world of space but that of time. "The wildest and
most extravagant fancies. . . of the lover, the madman, and
the poet" contain a high order of truth:

Not all unreal is the bright world of Romance into which we
rise from the dull Actual in all our moments of higher and
intenser life. The "land of dreams," in which the lover and the
poet, in their intensest frenzy, rise free and delighted, is, if we
did but know it, more substantial than this cold, dry, work-day
world, in which for the most part of the time we merely vegetate, and call it living. In these moments the soul penetrates
beyond the Actual to the Ideal, which is the basis of all reality,
that in which we are all, without seeming to know it, immersed
as in a vast ocean of being.[22]

This is a far cry from the idea of imagination afforded by
Common Sense thought, nowhere so different as in its
implications for art. And the difference arises out of the
respective metaphysical positions of Brownson and the Scottish realists: the latter, as we have seen, defined the order of
possibility as dependent on and inferior to the order of
actuality. Brownson, on the other hand, idealizes the possible
order and makes the actual depend on the ideal. Within the
actual, sustaining it, as it were, is the ideal. To know the
ideal, existing objectively as such, is to know more about
the nature of reality. And it is by means of the imagination
that we are best able to get "through" the actual to the
ideal. Thus the poet or artist, expressing what he has perceived after he has gotten "through," performs a laudable
function, for he explores reality more thoroughly and more
deeply than the great majority of persons, who, indeed, de-

pend upon him for all but the more obvious and common knowledge. "The only real instructor of the human race is the artist," states Brownson, "and it is as artists, as men wrought up to the intensest life, and therefore acting from the full force of their being, that Socrates, Plato, Descartes, the great and universally admitted philosophers, have been able to quicken the race, and set it forward to a higher and more comprehensive life." Art is sacred; the highest truths come from the imaginations of men; for "no man is really a philosopher till warmed into the artist."[23]

Brownson's objective idealism thus departs radically in statement and implication from the principles of Scottish realism. And the idealisms of such men as Emerson, Thoreau, and Whitman mark equally decisive departures in their efforts to get beyond the limitations of empiricism and common sense by insisting on the value of what lies within. "The poet is he who can best see and best say what is ideal," said James Russell Lowell in 1855; the poet stands for the imagination, protecting the world from "blank materialism." Emphasizing the need for wonder and for loyalty to the dreams of our youth, Lowell believes that Americans can conquer the future only by moral greatness, ideas, and works of imagination. He admits that his is an age of common sense, but advocates the imagination on the grounds that it is "the common sense of the invisible world"—a striking definition, which tries bluntly and perhaps wishfully to reconcile two faculties which a culture had proposed as irreconcilable. Committed ultimately to an invisible world of some kind, the transcendentalist would feel it necessary to break through to reality; what was immediately available in the world around him was not enough, since it merely covered or symbolized a reality of greater value. And whether he broke through by going inward or outward to ideality depended on the reality structure to which he gave allegiance. In either case, the desire for a higher, more intense reality demanded concepts of the imagination as a creative power that were remote from the fundamental principles of Common Sense philosophy.

All this is not to imply that the Scots had no use for the imagination. Although it presented being of an inferior order, although it was liable to excess and required rigorous attention to be kept in its place, still it had a place; the imagination was part of the human make-up and had to be considered as such. Controlled and stabilized by reason, it could add a richness of texture to human life. Indeed, Dugald Stewart analyzed at some length the importance of the culture of imagination—his words serving, in effect, as advice to men living in a world which offers artistic pleasures and gratifications. Stewart's analysis reflects, moreover, the tension between his metaphysics and his position as a reasonable citizen of the world. What he offers is a kind of *modus vivendi*, a way of enjoying the pleasures of imagination without abrogating the rule of reason.

The highest function of the imagination, says Stewart, lies in its faculty of creation, or—and he puts it "more correctly" from his and the Common Sense point of view—in its faculty "of invention and new combination." But because he wishes to consider man's ability to appreciate the imaginative endeavors of others rather than man's capacity for invention, Stewart distinguishes between the apprehensive and the inventive powers of imagination, the apprehensive power relating to taste and involving the appreciation of inventions and combinations. (It is interesting and, I think, instructive that such men as Coleridge, Emerson, and Brownson stress the active and creative aspect of art, and feature the role of the artist, whereas Stewart pays little attention to the artist and is at his most persuasive when dealing with the passive or appreciative aspect of art.) With reference to this apprehensive power, he advocates a "judicious culture" of taste that must begin with the culture of the imagination and depend further on association and other intellectual processes. Stewart puts it in strong language: if man is not to be "incomplete and mutilated," he must cultivate the apprehensive power of his imagination.[24]

But the imagination must be cultivated under "the wholesome discipline of rules"; reason and good sense, steadily exercised, will control, guide, and stimulate this "important, but subordinate faculty." Stewart does not hold the imagination and the intellect to be antipathetic (which really means here that he advocates a taste formed by intelligence); on the contrary, the intellect can be a great aid to imaginative appreciation. As an example, he points out that the English poet Dr. Mark Akenside had a much keener appreciation of a rainbow after he had studied Newton's theory of light and color. "According to the common doctrine," as Stewart knows, a gradual decline of imaginative vitality "after the short season of youth, is not merely the natural consequence of growing reason and experience, but the necessary effect of our physical organization!" An analogous notion, "commonly, or rather universally taught of late," holds that the imagination is most perfect in rude or primitive societies, "when the faculties shoot up wild and free."[25] But Stewart, entering a minority view (as Lord Kames had done before him) in his desire to allow for what we might call imaginative intelligence, objects to both these concepts. He does not exalt the childish or the primitive imagination, and it is his commitment to reason rather than to the imagination that prompts him to demur. Granted that the child is easily led into fairylands of adventure; as he matures, if reason is not brought to bear as a guiding principle to give him intellectual grounds for taste, his imagination may run to excess, and then, paradoxically, dry up. Stewart manages to express his belief in the culture of the imagination and his always latent suspicion of imaginative activity at the same time by saying that a lively imagination is almost invariably united "with a weak judgment, with scanty stores of acquired knowledge, and with little industry to supply the defect." As a consequence, "the materials, which it is the province of imagination to modify and combine, are soon exhausted; the internal resourses [sic] of reason and meditation are wanting; and the imagination either disappears altogether, or degenerates into childishness and folly."[26] A lively imagination is one thing; an imagination that is lively because it is suffused by reason is something else again, and much better. Not even the most enthusiastic schoolboy can appreciate Virgil or Milton in the manner of a person of "cultivated taste and an enlightened understanding."[27] Reason thus heightens the apprehensive power of the imagination and also introduces duration to its pleasures—both to the individual experience of pleasure and to one's general capacity for imaginative enjoyment.

What is true individually, argues Stewart, is true culturally. In a primitive society, to be sure, the imagination is vigorous and unchecked. Much to be preferred, however, are the productions of genius "disciplined by an enlightened taste"—the "noblest efforts of imagination."[28] Stewart defines the cultivated imagination as that "which has acquired such a degree of activity as to delight in its own exertions."[29] It affords excursions into the regions of fancy analogous to those of foreign travel; from both we return home; both are enveloped by the familiar realities of actual, everyday life. "For my own part," says Stewart, praising reason and not primitivism,

I think I can now enjoy these tales of wonder with as lively a relish as the most credulous devotee in the superstitious times which gave them birth: Nor do I value the pleasure which they afford me the less, that my reason teaches me to regard them as vehicles of amusement, not as articles of faith.—But it is not *reason* alone that operates, in an age like the present, in correcting the credulity of our fore-fathers. Imagination herself furnishes the most effectual of all remedies against those errors of which she was, in the first instance, the cause; the versatile activity which she acquires by constant and varied exercise, depriving superstition of the most formidable engine it was able heretofore to employ, for subjugating the infant understanding. In proportion to the number and diversity of the objects to which she turns her attention, the dangers are diminished which are apt to arise from her illusions, when they are suffered always to run in the same channel. . . .[30]

Thus Stewart commends the cultivated imagination, which can withdraw into a world of its own making, but which can dismiss this world at the proper moment to return to affairs of a more important because more real nature. Controlled, under the sanction of a ruling intelligence, the imagination may add a desirable dimension of pleasure to human life.

Stewart's discussion of the culture of the imagination, so very reasonable and commonsensical in its approach to the subject, demonstrates a way of coming to terms with it. With no shifting of his basic metaphysical position, which defined possible reality as ontologically inferior to actual reality, he is able to view the imagination as an important but subordinate faculty. This ability to afford the grounds for a militant objection to imaginative experience and at the same time to take a more sophisticated and sweetly reasonable view of its controlled operation under the heading of taste further suggests the plastic appeal of Common Sense thought. It offered something to practically everyone—except the creative artist.

In Quest of Fiction

The American fictive imagination would strive toward creation largely in the context of a mechanist conception of the
imagination and the Scottish metaphysic, with a deriva-
tive and practical emphasis on social and moral stability. If
there had to be fiction, it ought to be fiction controlled and
made safe in its turn, fiction as a kind of social-moral agent.
Some American fiction would follow this presumptive pattern, though what we have come to regard as our significant
fiction would result from different attempts at creation.

The simplest and most immediate method of control was
to be didactic, to take the principles of social and moral
organization and bring them to bear as the reality principle
on the assembled world of the novel. The bulk of early
American fiction is professedly didactic, the novels of
Susanna Rowson, for example, or Hannah Webster Foster's
The Coquette (1797), or Caroline Matilda Warren Thayer's
The Gamester's (1805), or Sukey Vickery's *Emily Hamilton* (1803). And at times, as in the case of Tabitha Tenney's
Female Quixotism (1801), we find novels mocking novels—
a case of the controlled imagination scorning and satirizing
and hence reducing the threat of the very idea of fiction.

Susanna Rowson, however, stands as the most thoroughly
and effectively didactic of these early writers. Employing
the conventions of the sentimental novel, she molds her material into dramatized patterns of instruction. The didactic
precision of her imagination admits nothing into the world
of her novels that will not ultimately support the idea that
morality is the sole means to happiness in life (for Mrs.
Rowson, a moral purpose measures even novelistic success):
selection of theme, portrayal of character, narration of incident, style, tone,—all are selected and shaped for the purpose
of teaching this lesson. That fiction so conceived and exe-

cuted could achieve eminent popularity is proved beyond doubt by *Charlotte Temple* (1791; first American edition 1794), the first perennial best-seller in American fiction, which went through some 158 editions, the last in 1905.[31] Fiction for Mrs. Rowson was a vehicle of instruction; when she began her school for girls in Boston she announced her retirement as a novelist, apparently having less time and less inclination to write novels now that she could teach directly.[32]

Not all writers were able to suffuse their books with didacticism to the degree that Mrs. Rowson could. The tacked-on and interpolated statement of moral intent, suggested additionally by its prevalence in eighteenth-century English fiction but distinctively sharper and more insistent than its English counterpart, came to be a characteristic of the early American novel—what we might consider a kind of pseudo-didacticism. And it covered a multitude of sins. Far from being cramped by his mode of creation (or invention), the pseudo-didactic novelist achieved a kind of release. Under the dispensation of a reality principle of didacticism, he could indulge his imagination (fancy, in Coleridge's sense) to the utmost, constructing or assembling bizarre fictive worlds. Beneath the moralistic-didactic surface of much early American fiction lies a world of wretchedness. It is a world in which seduction, incest, and broken lives scream out, but the screams are muted. What emerges is a controlled, as it were didactic terror—ideally, just terrifying enough to make the reader content to be living in the actual world. These novels, for the most part, are domestic, because the integrity and solidarity of the family—the essential unit of society—are at stake. They are sentimental, because, as Helen W. Papashvily remarks in *All the Happy Endings*, sentimentality "is always a cloak to hide the face of horror." Popular and numerous, they show us one manner in which a didactic principle of literary creation could serve the writer's imagination.

A number of early American novels defy rigid classification as they attempt to fuse such things as ideas of human progress, sentiments of patriotism, and conventions of minor English fiction into some sort of novelistic whole. When the fusion fails, the result is a work puzzling in form; such books, I believe, are best considered "sports." Henry Sherburne's *Oriental Philanthropist* (1800), for example, brings the contemporarily faddish Gothic interest in the East together with a utopian scheme of government; Oriental fairy-tale machinery helps to constitute the ideal state. According to formula, Sherburne hopes that his work will instill "active principles of piety, virtue, and benevolence" into the human heart, since (the formula takes on specific application) these are "the only and sure foundation of civil, social and domestic felicity." He disclaims artistic talent, invokes didactic and patriotic motives, and adds a touch of the millenial. "O happy country," he says to (or of) America, where all realize the momentous influence of morality on progress. Significantly, his utopia will have no fiction, for "genuine unmixed truth shall shine forth with charms superceding the necessity of the fascinating blandishments of fictitious tales." The direction of Sherburne's argument suggests a Platonic objection to poetry, an objection encased in and adapted to national concerns, although the suggestion remains vague in the resolution of the book. Fiction is necessary because of the imperfect condition of the world; paradoxically, fiction will work toward its own extinction, for the progress leading to the millenium will refine it out of existence. Nevertheless, adds Sherburne, "works of imagination, when subservient to reason and virtue, will never fail to be admired."[33]

Samuel Woodworth's *The Champions of Freedom; or*

The Mysterious Chief (1816), a story dealing with the War of 1812, contains what must be one of the most elaborate prefaces ever written for a novel. Woodworth presents his preface in a dramatic framework consisting of a dialogue between a critical friend and himself concerning the merits of his manuscript. When the friend asks "what useful end can possibly be attained" by the publication of the work, the author quotes from his Advertisement: "The grand object intended by the work here announced to the public, is a monument of American patriotism and bravery, embellished with a picture of those humbler virtues, which, though not so dazzling to the imagination, are not the less honorable to human nature and our national character." When the friend objects to "absurd" incidents in the tale, Woodworth replies that "the absurdity of the *incidents* must not be imputed to me; . . . they are all copied from life—most of them are historically correct." Woodworth acknowledges that his "pertinacity in adhering to matters of fact, combined with the very nature of the subject, has introduced more agents on the stage than would be welcome in a work of mere imagination." He hopes the reader will pardon this "on the grounds just premised, viz. the impossibility of avoiding it without a violation of fact." Moreover, although the story is "embellished with a few fictitious scenes, incidents, and characters, it will, nevertheless, be the most correct and complete History of the recent War, that has yet appeared." In an apparent effort to please all types of readers, Woodworth expresses the hope that the book "will be found equally interesting, as a history or a novel" and that the "lovers of each will find themselves pleasantly led from one to another of their own favorite scenes, without a very wearisome march through those of their opponents in taste."[34]

Both books make it obvious that their writers have no

viable concept of fiction. Sherburne assembles or constructs the world of his novel out of three general elements: the machinery of the Eastern fairy tale, the notion of a benevolent man, and the idea of utopia. The manner in which he puts these elements together into a novel exemplifies, I believe, the inventive process of the mechanist imagination. But the job of assembling is crude; *The Oriental Philanthropist* becomes a personalized tract employing the imaginary or possible as a fixed, static entity. Confused in conception and execution, the book is surest when it posits fiction as a subject for discussion, when, that is, it foresees the happy doom of fiction. The final concession that works of imagination deserve admiration "when subservient to reason and virtue" anticipates Stewart's argument on the culture of imagination and echoes the prevailing attitude of essays, sermons, and speeches concerning the danger of imaginative indulgence.

Woodworth's *The Champions of Freedom* is especially interesting here because of the manner in which it fails to cohere as a fictional unit. We are back at the beginnings of American historical fiction in *The Champions;* we sense from it the almost insurmountable problems inherent in the writing of such fiction until Scott and then Cooper demonstrated how it could be done. For this is a book with a split personality, a false start toward historical fiction. History for Woodworth is one thing, fiction another; he cannot bring the two together. The most he can do is arrange them side by side in episodes and hope that his book will be read "as a history or a novel." In the terms of our earlier analysis we may say that Woodworth's fundamental dilemma is metaphysical, involving his conception of history and fiction as two different kinds of reality; history is actual and hence superior, fiction is possible and hence inferior. Thus conceived, history and fiction cannot be fused into an artistic

whole. That Woodworth would fail in the attempt is for
us as historians after-the-fact predictable; that he should
even try is the point worth noting. He is attempting to conceive something counter to his essential attitude toward
reality, something, therefore, which he has not the means of
conceiving. This is not to say that a man striving toward
artistic creation cannot overcome basic counter attitudes; it
takes a great deal more talent, however, than Woodworth
possessed (and thus we come to a way of defining his mani-
fest limitations). Perhaps aware of a fundamental confusion
of motive in *The Champions*, Woodworth ends his preface
on a note of personal humility that is arrestingly simple after
his elaborate earlier contrivings. Regarding the "execution"
of his plans, he has little to say: "It is my first attempt, and
I have done the best I could. In many respects I have studied
the interest of the reader alone, by making short para-
graphs, and lessening the length of a chapter when the
subject is dull, and increasing it when the incidents are interesting." The statement lies open to ridicule, but we laugh
at it in a humor of embarrassment. In fact, we may come to
know a great deal more about what it was to write fiction
in early nineteenth-century America by understanding how
it was that Woodworth wrote as he did.

A "sport" of a different kind is William Hill Brown's
Ira and Isabella, published posthumously in 1807. Although
Brown's *The Power of Sympathy* has gained some attention
as the first American novel, *Ira and Isabella* has gone practically unnoticed. Indeed, it invites neglect: in this over-
wrought, sentimentalized narrative the orphans ("natural
children") Ira and Isabella fall in love, decide to marry, discover they are brother and sister, resign themselves to a suitable affection, discover they are *not* brother and sister, and
finally marry. Yet in a surprising, adventitious, and clumsy
way the novel addresses the problems of writing fiction in

early America. For Brown is both aware and articulate; while Sherburne and Woodworth fail mutely, Brown fails in an avalanche of rhetoric that reveals a shrewd self-consciousness of himself as a writer coupled with occasional provocative insights into the nature of his society. Capable of irony, capable of toying with some of the most basic assumptions of his culture, he at once questions and employs the conventions of writing sentimental fiction.

The surprises of *Ira and Isabella* begin with the subtitle, "A Novel Founded in Fiction."[35] Balanced against this bold, possibly ironic, and unique assertion is an epigraph from the Scottish rhetorician Hugh Blair containing a more orthodox notion. "Fictitious histories," says Blair, "might be employed for very useful purposes. They furnish one of the best channels for conveying instruction; for painting human life and manners; for showing the errors into which we are betrayed by our passions; for rendering virtue amiable, and vice odious." We have, thus, an avowed fiction with a moral purpose, not a novel founded in "fact" or "truth" which itself serves as the basis of instruction. In his lengthy preface, Brown joins with Marmontel in lamenting the loss of "fairyism," without which the task of writing fiction demands a far greater thoroughness of invention. Brown regrets "the loss of machinery in modern novels"; he grieves "most of all. . . for the extinction of the eastern manner" in which he could have displayed himself "in all my glory." "There could I have fired away in periods sonorous, lofty, musical and unmeaning, and proved myself a Confucius or Xixzoffou by the orientality of sentiments, grand, obscure, magnificent and incomprehensible. Genii and giants, magii and magicians, invincible castles and palaces of enchantment, should have spontaneously arisen from one stroke of my immortal wand." Brown apparently enjoys his rhetoric: "the perverse fashion of the present day" bars his path "to glory, honour and to a long list of convenient et-caeteras."[36] Though it is difficult to be certain of the prevailing tone of many of his remarks, he seems to be having a good time. Nonetheless, he is stating baldly the basic problem of artistic creation in a new country which could offer no traditional body of story stuff for the writer to work with, in which the burden of creation came to be on the individual imagination. In his *English Traits* (1856), Emerson commented that every Englishman is "a thousand years old and lives by his memory." But Brown, as an American, feels completely on his own, "unwarrantably forbidden. . . to introduce fairies and enchanters as a help to. . . make a book." Even the assistance of the heathen mythology of Rosicrucianism (this perhaps referring to "The Rape of the Lock") is denied him.

The story itself investigates "the metaphysicks of misfortune"—principally the trials of Ira and Isabella when they believe themselves to be brother and sister. Isabella consistently advocates " 'stability of character,' " judging it to be an important virtue. In turn, " 'I will be stable,' " says Ira, "with firmness." Exhorting Ira to morality and religion, Isabella comments that " 'stability is the offspring of a serious mind' "; she strikes the stylized pose of exhortation that features numerous illustrations in novels of the eighteenth and nineteenth centuries: "her posture was firm, and her eye fixed upon her brother; her right hand placed upon her breast, and her left pointing toward heaven." The rake Florio, however, who "had turned over more pages of novels than of Roman history," urges Ira to live, not to vegetate. He desires to get a *"knowledge of the world"*; his " 'notion of existence' " is to " 'live all the days of our life.' "

Much later, in the fiction of Henry James, this idea of living one's life would become a basic and highly wrought theme. But for James, "living" involves the discrimination of experience; for Brown and other early American novel-

ists, as well as for most of their successors until the time of
James, "living" is a general invitation to licentiousness.
Thus the protestations of morality and stability, the puri-
tanical fear of "living," the morality of abstention, as Philip
Rahv calls it, all capable of being reinforced and given an
intellectual pedigree by the philosophy of Common Sense
with its own qualities of stability, conservatism, and security. But stability, of course, affords its own principles for
the discrimination of experience; negative in many ways,
discouraging the autonomy of imaginative experience, they
are the primary though unstressed heritage we have from
this America.

Brown demonstrates his independence of novelistic convention near the end of *Ira and Isabella* by going out of his
way to tell us that Lucinda, Ira's unwed mother (who does
not even appear in the novel), "did not find it in her heart
to die out of complaisance" to the moral opinions of the age.
Other writers may "presume it for the interest of morality
to represent misfortune and death as the consequences of
indiscretion." But Lucinda, "notwithstanding her slip," secured an honest, industrious husband. No enemy to morality, but no "professed dealer in literature," Brown wants
only "to speak the truth"—a truth, if we recall the novel's
subtitle, founded in fiction. This first American claim to
fictional truth, undercut by the probability that Brown is
for some reason (most likely satiric) making up for his insistence on the tragic effects of seduction in *The Power
of Sympathy*, remained private for over fourteen years until
the publication of the novel. It seems more a gesture of
defiance than a genuine commitment to fictional truth and
to the possible as an instrument of that truth. But the verbal
claim is there at least, for whatever reasons. More than most
of his contemporaries, Brown seems to have thought, with
some sporadic success, about the nature of the novel. He

would not presume to design "a new creation of super-natural agents" to replace those now forbidden; yet he says that the novel needs "a novel machinery"—something new and for itself. He seems to have realized that the novel required a new and special kind of imaginative creation, although he was unable to define or show specifically what this might involve. He was, however, shrewd enough to see an important relation between the novel and love: "There is one truth concerning novels, which is in our time pretty well established; none I presume will controvert the authenticity of my remark, that the foundation of these elegant fabricks is laid on the passion of love. I except the wonderful history of Robinson Crusoe."[37] An insight of this sort, an epigraph from Blair, a unique subtitle, amateurish characterization, an almost complete lack of temporal-spatial setting, an overdone plot, an allusive and playful manner—such things merged into one book constitute the oddity of *Ira and Isabella*.[38]

It has long been obvious to us that these early American writers produced distinctly sub-literary fiction; we may even perceive what was evidently not so obvious to them, the principal condition of their failure—more primary than a relative innocence of technique—the lack of a valid concept of fiction. For concept comes first; from it derives technique. The thoroughly and pre-eminently didactic fiction of Susanna Rowson leads one relentlessly, if patiently, toward the world of fact and history, matching, as it were, the movement of her own career from actress to didactic novelist to schoolmistress. The writers whom I have called pseudo-didactic indulged themselves in little orgies of imagination under the dispensation of an adventitious, educative premise. The writer of "sports" questioned the very conventions to which he perforce gave allegiance. The general result was a body of "fiction" so earnest in its concern to succeed that it strikes us as funny and thus impresses us only as an abortive early chapter in the history of the American literary imagination.

The Romance

Paradoxical as it may seem at first glance, there was no lack of imaginative experience in early American fiction—that is, if we measure quantitatively. The problem, indeed, can be said to be one of quantity, of overabundance. But this is, after all, what we might expect, for in a large sense there has never been any lack of imagination in America (or perhaps anywhere else). We have only to look at the sermons of Jonathan Edwards or the political writings of Jefferson, Hamilton, or Madison to see how metaphor could be used to structure and dramatize the need for sincere repentance or to argue the causes of statecraft; these men move easily beyond the techniques of literal argument to an idiom conceived imaginatively, yet naturally; they consistently employ the stylistics of imaginative persuasion as means to definite ends which, in turn, generate enough intensity to evoke suitable stylistic forms in minds otherwise capable of severe literalness.[39] And since sheer intensity of belief in the desirability of a natural or supernatural goal is not of itself a sufficient explanation for what they achieved, we must credit these men with a special kind of talent or genius. Although the attempted creation of a more thoroughly sustained imaginative object poses issues of a different nature (so that the poetics of salvation or federation are not those of fiction), we may say that the novelist in early America also faced the problem of finding the means to an end. The end (perhaps dimly seen at times) was to create literature as belles-lettres, that is, to explore the possibilities of human action in society; the means were of course to imagine human experience, to imagine people thinking, feeling, and acting. As we all know, this had been done, at times with difficulty, with varying degrees of success, throughout the history of Western civilization, so that there was no dearth of example for the would-be American writer of fiction. But even to say this is to oversimplify by implication, for to suggest that Americans could avail themselves at will of their Western heritage is grossly to neglect history. What had been done imaginatively in other nations had not been done in America; and the history of our early literature demonstrates the extreme difficulty of accommodating the general example of Western culture to a new set of particular, individuating, and hence identifying circumstances.[40] The achievement of such men as Edwards and Jefferson had long directed the imaginative resources of the American mind to Puritan-national concerns; historically, Americans had enlisted in the causes of God and country. The effects of such direction were present in early nineteenth-century America, making it cumulatively difficult to achieve a new kind of investment and release for the imagination. Moreover, as we have seen, a more or less select, a judicial group of Americans (historically formed, let us note, by the persistent importance of belief in God and country to which intellectual, imaginative, and emotional energies had been, as it were, indentured) was increasingly influenced by the Scottish Common Sense philosophers, from whom they would learn a metaphysic that preferred actuality and denigrated possibility—a rational, reasonable, significantly up-to-date body of thought that would encourage them to think as they were already prone to think.

American writers invented their fiction under the aegis of this philosophy and imagined human thought, feeling, and action accordingly; they created, that is, a body of imaginary experience that needed no quantitative bounds. But in the absence of what Perry Miller in another context calls the proper stratagems of consciousness the created imaginative experience threatened always to run ahead of suitable forms for that experience. For the task of the writer was (and is) to create formed experience—the question of meaning cannot be separated from the question of form. The forms of theological and political expression were not, of course, suitable for the writer of fiction. We have seen the attempts of some early writers to discover novelistic form in the principles of social-moral organization; but when these principles were themselves ultimately anti-fictive, the inadequacy of such attempts was at the very least highly probable. The result was either a thoroughly didactic fiction such as that of Mrs. Rowson, fiction as lesson, or a pseudo-didactic exercise in how much the imagination could invent, contained in and by the flimsy borrowed form of the sentimental novel.[41] Not to appropriate form in this way, however, was to run the risk of writing "sports," in which one sees only the fragments of form. The crudely formed experience in early American fiction, integrally related to the prevailing concept of the status of fiction, derived finally from the general suspicion of the imaginative order, which one might defy, but hardly with artistic impunity.

We may formulate a complementary and, I believe, helpful description of this relationship between fiction and culture. Because of a pervasive emphasis on the necessity of stability in social organization, social experience in the first decades of the nineteenth century came under a rigorous judicial scrutiny to a degree probably never surpassed in American history. Clergymen, educators, lawyers, men in public life—such men held or assumed the rights to a kind of priority of comment on what might affect, for good or for bad, the structure of the society they were still creating. That the whole structure, including themselves, was relatively insecure made them the more vigilant, the more bound to stress the implements of stability—one of which would be Scottish realism. It is in this light that we should consider James Marsh's statement that the leading principles of Locke and the Scottish writers had become so combined with religious belief that both appeared as necessary parts of the same system. Thus also the maverick Thomas Cooper's complaint against the centrality of Scottish thought or the militant call in the *North American Review's* laudatory review of Levi Frisbie's *Inaugural Address* for responsibility in the present as the way to future national glory. All such statements imply the existence of a social orthodoxy. Society was under a kind of management that invested social experience with grave public responsibility. And no significant aspect of this social experience could be compromised by attempts at novelistic expression; the novelist thus competed for material and forms with those who were molding and sustaining American society, but the experience that he wished to address resisted *transformation* into art until it had been given more complete *formation* as the bases of social existence.[42]

If American fiction could not readily be conceived and executed with success in the midst of a social organization seriously intent on its own structure, if a novelistic concern with society was thwarted or rendered difficult, there remained, as we know from our literary history, another way of creating fiction. It is not, strictly speaking, an alternative way, for the word "alternative" suggests a kind of conscious selection between obvious possibilities that is probably not historically accurate. There was, however, a way of less resistance, of creating more privately, of investigating in fiction a less socially prescribed internal experience.

To put the problem in these terms is immediately to recall the transcendental imagination. We have seen that such different transcendentalists as James Marsh, Emerson, Thoreau, and Brownson knew the philosophy of Common Sense as one of the props of conservatism and moved beyond what they considered its limitations toward the truths that lie deep within (to paraphrase Marsh). From their personal, intuitive quest for a higher reality we might, if we did not know better, expect the kind of imaginative insight that would issue forth as autonomous fictional experience, ignoring by simply transcending the strictures of society. Yet from these men came no body of fiction; the transcendental imagination did not dispose itself to fictional creation. As a form of idealism, transcendentalism would have an implicit case against fiction based loosely on the classic Platonic argument against poetry: if intuition and internal fact offered the purest reality, and if external fact was merely emblematic, then fictional fact would be an emblem of an emblem and would leave one two removes from true reality. From the transcendentalist came not so much a distrust of as a distaste for fiction. Emerson, we recall, admired Hawthorne the man, but thought his fiction unworthy of him. It is as if Emerson desired a far more primary kind of creation than fiction called for; Melville comments, for example, that the "gaping flaw" in Emerson ("this Plato who talks thro' his nose") is "the insinuation, that had he lived in those days when the world was made, he might have offered some valuable suggestions"; and Santayana, in a statement that stands interestingly with Melville's, says that Emerson "was like a young god making experiments in creation: he blotched the work, and always began again on a new and better plan."[43] Whitman, who may strike us as an even younger god than Emerson, sees fiction as inferior in genuineness to poetry. His particular objection to the romance derives from his objection to all caricature, especially that of the human form. "Great genius and the people of these states must

never be demeaned to romances," he wrote in his 1855
Preface to *Leaves of Grass:* "As soon as histories are properly
told there is no more need of romances." Intensely interested
in the creation of "new free forms," Whitman must inveigh
against the romance out of loyalty to his own discovery of
form in the person. Romance caricatures—Whitman ad-
mires, preserves, and glorifies; romance demeans—Whitman
dignifies; for the dignity of the "simple separate" person will
measure the dignity of his new free poetic form.

Thus, although the transcendentalists dealt with a kind
of experience not so readily capable of social prescription,
they did not form it into fiction. The most significant fiction
produced in America during the first half of the nineteenth
century made its appearance in and through the romance,
which Whitman criticized so specifically in 1855 because
it had already become a working tradition in American fiction. For the romance, too, dealt with private, internal experience—or with experience formed in a private, personal
manner. From our consideration of the morals and metaphysics of American society and of the conditions of novel-
writing in that society, we may come, I believe, to a fuller
understanding of the attractions that the romance held for
the American writer.

A distinction between the romance and the novel was
well established by the nineteenth century. As early as 1692
in his *Incognita*, Congreve had characterized the romance
as dealing with the wondrous and unusual and the novel as
depicting events of a more familiar nature—and we have seen
that Clara Reeve made the same distinction in 1785. With
some verbal adaptation but no basic change, this formula
remained intact in the nineteenth century, so that when
Hawthorne in 1851 distinguished between the two fictional
forms in his preface to *The House of Seven Gables*, he could
say he "need hardly" observe that the romance implies "a

certain latitude, both as to its fashion and material," not to
be found in the novel. The novel "is presumed to aim at a
very minute fidelity, not merely to the possible, but to the
probable and ordinary course of man's experience"; the
romance, while it must adhere to the truth of the human
heart, implies a greater freedom in presenting circumstances
and in managing the "atmospherical medium" so as to "bring
out or mellow the lights and deepen and enrich the shadows
of the picture." The writer of romance, that is, can select,
alter, and refract reality to form a world not in immediate
competition with the actual social world (but perhaps ultimately its most thorough and competent critic).

In his preface for *The American*, Henry James searches
out the essence of the romantic and of the romance, and, in
doing so, supplies what I believe is the crucial consideration
of the way in which the romance served the creative needs
of the earlier American writer. The strange and the far, says
James, are not necessarily romantic; they represent the un-
known which the increasing range of our experience may
convert into the known. Nor does a romantic temper in a
character constitute an essential aspect of romance (Emma
Bovary is thus a romantic, while "nothing less resembles a
romance" than *Madame Bovary*). The romance will always
explore a reality that "with all the facilities in the world, all
the wealth and all the courage and all the wit and all the
adventure, we never *can* directly know; the things that can
reach us only through the beautiful circuit and subterfuge
of our thought and our desire." Romance must deal with a
certain kind of reality (or what seems to me a certain manner of reality)—and here James comes to the crux of his
definition:

The only *general* attribute of projected romance that I can see,
the only one which fits all its cases, is the fact of the kind of

experience with which it deals—experience liberated, so to speak; experience disengaged, disembroiled, disencumbered, exempt from the conditions that we usually know to attach to it and, if we wish so to put the matter, drag upon it, and operating in a medium which relieves it, in a particular interest, of the inconvenience of a *related*, a measurable state, a state subject to all our vulgar communities.

Let us pause here momentarily, for the case for understanding the romance in its particular American setting could hardly be better put. The romance permitted the American writer to deal with experience without the "inconvenience" of relating it to his society, experience "exempt" from the manifold conditions of that society, experience liberated, "disengaged, disembroiled, disencumbered." It offered a way of meeting experience raw, personally, in an unformed state, and dealing with it in a fictional-artistic manner. It allowed the writer, in effect, to desocialize experience in an effort to validate it imaginatively, or, we might say, to approach reality presocially, exempt from social prescription. All this, of course, is a matter of degree, since some connection with, some relation to, society is always maintained. As James goes on to say, the greatest intensity in a romance is evidently arrived at "when the sacrifice of community, of the 'related' sides of situations, has not been too rash." The romance

must to this end not flagrantly betray itself; we must even be kept if possible, for our illusion, from suspecting any sacrifice at all. The balloon of experience is in fact of course tied to the earth, and under that necessity we swing, thanks to a rope of remarkable length, in the more or less commodious car of the imagination; but it is by the rope we know where we are, and from the moment that cable is cut we are at large and unrelated: we only swing apart from the globe—though remaining as exhilarated, naturally, as we like, especially when all goes well. The art of the romancer, is "for the fun of it," insidiously to cut the cable, to cut it without our detecting him.

We are, obviously, using James's statements heuristically here; they explain much about the creation of experience in the romance, yet no early American romancer possessed the same concern for refinement and technique. Not even Hawthorne, for example, puts much theoretic emphasis on a subtle cutting loose of the balloon of experience. The wise writer, he admits, will "mingle the Marvellous rather as a slight, delicate, and evanescent flavor, than as any portion of the actual substance of the dish offered to the public." But even if the writer disregard this caution, he can hardly be said to "commit a literary crime." And many earlier writers than Hawthorne cut their balloons loose with a vengeance, for in dealing with disengaged experience the writer perforce relied to a greater degree on the forming energy of his own imagination; if he lacked the proper discipline and inner control, the results could be monstrous in their own way—as in *Constantius and Pulchera* (1797), or *Julia and the Illuminated Baron* (1800), or *Alonzo and Melissa* (1811). This last book was well enough known for Mark Twain to include it among a table of books in *Life on the Mississippi;* but the fact that it placed a moat, a drawbridge, and a castle-like dwelling in an American setting shows to what extent the disencumbered and yet still mechanist imagination could go in the invention of assemblages.

The romance was no panacea for the would-be American writer; it introduced its own set of problems for him to overcome. But it did allow the fictive imagination to function in a "disengaged" and "disembroiled" manner; it did allow the writer to create experience without attaching the usual social conditions to that experience. The romance thus helped to liberate the American imagination from the essentially anti-fictive context of its society. It marked one more breaking away from the implications of Scottish metaphysics, for one who created fiction in the mode of romance assumed the validity of imaginative experience.

The Haunted Mind

We may illustrate the nature of the creative problem facing the American writer of fiction by considering Hawthorne's sketch "The Haunted Mind" in relation to James Beattie's instructions for dispersing the terrors of the night in his *Dissertations Moral and Critical*. Apparently using his aunt Mary Manning's share in the Salem Athenaeum, Hawthorne read a good deal of the Scots in 1827, two years after his graduation from Bowdoin; between April and August of that year he withdrew from the library Kames's *Sketches of the History of Man* and *Elements of Criticism*, Thomas Brown's *Lectures on the Philosophy of the Human Mind*, Stewart's *Philosophical Essays*, and Alison's *Essays on the Nature and Principles of Taste;* in November he again withdrew Kames's *Sketches*.[44] So that he knew not only of the existence of the Scots, but something of their thought, during the years of solitude following his graduation.

In "The Haunted Mind," Hawthorne writes of an hour in the night when one awakens suddenly and finds himself awake in a world of dreams. It is a time when "yesterday has already vanished among the shadows of the past" and "to-morrow has not yet emerged from the future, . . . an intermediate space, where the business of life does not intrude; where the passing moment lingers, and becomes truly the present." Father Time, thinking himself unobserved, sits down at this hour "to take breath." "Oh, that he would fall asleep," writes Hawthorne, "and let mortals live on without growing older." One looks through the partially frosted window into the cold clear world, shivers, and retreats head and all under the covers, for "it is too cold even for the thoughts to venture abroad." A speculation on the luxury of living forever like an oyster in a shell, "content with the sluggish ecstasy of inaction," brings by association a "hideous" idea "in its train"—that of the dead "lying in their cold shrouds and narrow coffins." That "gloomy thought will collect a gloomy multitude" of thoughts.

Employing a metaphor which he uses to advantage in probing the character of Judge Pyncheon in *The House of the Seven Gables*, Hawthorne writes that "in the depths of every heart there is a tomb and a dungeon, though the lights, the music, and revelry above may cause us to forget their existence, and the buried ones, or prisoners, whom they hide. But sometimes, and oftenest at midnight, these dark receptacles are flung wide open. In an hour like this, . . . the mind has a passive sensibility, but no active strength; . . . the imagination is a mirror, imparting vividness to all ideas, without the power of selecting or controlling them." Shame and guilt arise from the dungeon with an "indistinct horror of the mind." Breaking from "a sort of conscious sleep," you gaze "wildly round the bed, as if the fiends were anywhere but in your haunted mind." Embers on the hearth call up ideas of a different kind, which you enjoy "on the borders of sleep and wakefulness." Perhaps there is a parallel between human life and such an hour: "In both you emerge from mystery, pass through a vicissitude that you can but imperfectly control, and are borne onward to another mystery."

In his *Dissertations Moral and Critical*, James Beattie describes what he considers the most preferable way of handling "imaginary terrors" of the night. "By the glimmering of the moon," he writes, "I have once and again beheld, at midnight, the exact form of a man or woman, sitting silent and motionless by my bedside. Had I hid my head, without daring to look the apparition in the face, I should have passed the night in horror, and risen in the morning with the persuasion of having seen a ghost. But, rousing myself, and resolving to find out the truth, I discovered, that it was nothing more than the accidental disposition of my clothes upon a chair." On another occasion he was alarmed to see "by the faint light of the dawn, a coffin laid out between my bed and the window. I started up, and recollecting, that I had heard of such things having been seen by others, I set myself to examine it, and found it was only a stream of yellowish light, falling in a particular manner upon the floor, from between the window-curtains."[45]

Here we have two ways of dealing with the imagination at its most exacerbated. James Beattie has no place for the haunted mind: he will investigate and get at the facts of perception so that the actual world is re-established around him. If one looks at clothes on a chair, reasons Beattie in effect, and thinks he sees an apparition, there is a momentary conflict of reality. Investigation, however, proves the reality of the extramental world, leaving one to smile at the idea that was only in his mind. Such a simple illustration tells us much of the kind of impress Scottish thought made on the American imagination; even the terrors of the night could be made safe and explained away. There need be no haunted minds.

Hawthorne, however, speaks of the haunted mind as the basis of artistic creation; in his sketch he writes of the hour of creation on "the borders of sleep and wakefulness"; creation comes from a kind of "conscious sleep." Fiends rise up, but they are not to be found in the room, for they exist within the haunted mind. The imagination, we note, is passive, lacking the power of controlling its creations in a normal, daylight way. Such a method of using the imagination is distinctly opposed to the method employed by the Scots. The imagination in Hawthorne's sketch supplies a different kind of reality that must be dealt with on its own terms. In the "haunted mind" the imagination ceases to be subservient to literal fact, and the term is, I believe, a convenient metaphor for explaining the effectiveness of what we consider to be the best in American fiction—the work of Charles Brockden Brown and Poe and, with increasing depth and control, that of Hawthorne and Melville—up to the time of the Civil War.

It is easy for our sympathies to be enlisted here, for us to applaud the artistic endeavor which strove for true imaginative creation against the pervasive restrictions of the Common Sense philosophy and esthetic. To be honest with our own history, however, we must include in our focus the fact that Americans (committed to maintaining the stability of the social order) were largely suspicious of the implications of validating imaginative experience and that they had the Scottish philosophy from which to quote chapter and verse. We can see without difficulty that as a philosophy of containment Scottish realism could not but be temporary; our responsibility, however, is also to see that as a philosophy of stability it could not but be necessary. Perhaps, indeed, Scottish realism, even as it hindered the American writer's approach to the novelistic, forced him—if he had courage and genius enough—toward the romance. Perhaps, that is, Scottish realism built better than it knew when it constrained American writers to build otherwise.

4

A NOTE ON SOCIETY AND
THE IMAGINATION

Chapter Four

SINCE some American writers of fiction were not only aware of the resources of the romance as they employed them but theorized explicitly about its characteristics, it is virtually impossible that any examination of American fiction should not take account of the romance in some way. Needing the wild and the wonderful, says William Gilmore Simms in his preface to *The Yemassee*, the romance is not bound to the known or even to the probable: it differs from the novel in material and treatment and "grasps at the possible." And Hawthorne, in his famous preface to *The House of the Seven Gables*, says that when a writer calls his work a romance he need hardly lay claim to the imaginative latitude to which the form entitles him, so well known is the meaning of the term.

As we might expect, then, recent studies of American fiction have given a necessary attention to the romance and to the kinds of experience with which it has seemed especially equipped to deal. Truth in the romance, as Roy Harvey Pearce points out, is, at its best, general and operative; characters, situations, and settings are fashioned extravagantly, though all must be grounded in "local fact"— the general must be known in and through the particular.[1] From the relationship obtaining between general truth and particular fact would emerge a dependence on symbol as a crucial element in the romance. Charles Feidelson, Jr., has amply shown that symbolism is "the coloration taken on by the American literary mind under the pressure of American history"; in fiction, the chief symbolic vehicle was the romance.[2] Commenting that the American imagination seems, historically, to have been both embarrassed and obsessed by the "idyllic virginity of the terrain," Harry Levin also comes to see the romance as the "traditional medium of American fiction."[3]

The most fully developed analysis of the part played by the romance in American fiction is provided by Richard Chase in *The American Novel and Its Tradition* (1957). Mr. Chase expounds the thesis that "the American novel, in its most original and characteristic form, has worked out its destiny and defined itself by incorporating an element of romance."[4] Mr. Chase sees American culture as composed of "radical disunities," "contradictories," and "irreconcilables" which have their historical sources in the solitary position of man in this country, the Manichean quality of New England Puritanism, and the dual allegiance of the American to an old and to a new world. In its response to the "various pressures" of our culture, American fiction has departed from the novelistic tradition and worked out a romance-novel form of its own. The thesis itself can come as no surprise to the student of American fiction, who has become accustomed to noting the importance of the romance in the development of our fiction. But Mr. Chase extends his thesis beyond the Civil War and into the twentieth century in a way that will probably shape discussion of the American novel for some time to come. Romance, as all agree, implies the deliberate refraction of reality (the managing of one's atmospherical medium, in Hawthorne's phrase); but there are, of course, many possible angles of refraction. Implicit in the literary technique of naturalism is a principle of refraction, different from that of, say, Hawthorne, it is true, but nonetheless capable of presenting a carefully managed rather than a carefully reported reality. The existence of such a principle, Mr. Chase believes, has made it possible for American writers to continue to explore the resources of the romance for their own purposes and artistic needs (and so we get a phenomenon such as Frank Norris' "romance of the gutter"); thereby they have continued to work within an American tradition in the novel.

Any valid discussion of American fiction thus encounters the romance as a distinctive and significant fact which must somehow be taken into account. My concern here has been to enlarge our understanding of the historical emergence of the romance, or, more precisely, the concept of romance, as a way of writing fiction in the early United States. By considering the problem of fictional creation in its relation to the American suspicion of the imagination—an inherited Puritan mistrust fortified by the metaphysics of Common Sense philosophy—and by examining some of the abortive attempts to conceive and execute fiction in the early nineteenth century, we come, I believe, to see more fully and more surely the ways in which the romance served the American literary imagination.

Mistrust of the imagination and hostility toward fiction were not, of course, restricted to Americans. "A practical bent of mind, deep respect for facts, pragmatic skill in the adaption of means to ends, a ready appeal to common sense—and therefore, negatively, an indifference to abstract speculation and imaginative perception"—these are things which Walter E. Houghton enumerates as constant characteristics of the English people.[5] That the terms might also describe the American people points up the fact of a powerful Anglo-American tradition, on which the Scottish philosophy exercised a common influence. In England there

existed the same suspicion of the "blandishments of imaginative literature," particularly of the novel, that we have
found in the United States; there was the same kind of
attack on the novel as a purveyor of unreality. From English
Puritanism and contemporary neoclassicism came the means
of expression for this hostility.[6] But although the two nations shared the same attitude toward fiction, there is, I believe, a difference in the meaning of the attitude in the
respective societies.

In eighteenth-century England, as Richard D. Altick
indicates, "opposition to fiction on religious and moral principles became a convenient stalking-horse for other motives
which it was becoming less politic to avow."[7] Among these
less avowable motives was one with significant social implication, a feeling that the lower classes should not be taught,
or at least not be encouraged, to read. Because of what Mr.
Altick calls "a rigid, ineffaceable association of the mass
reading public with low-grade fiction" the novel was a prime
target for those who would keep the lower classes in their
places. Such critics discouraged learning, and not simply
the reading of novels, for the poor, and their idea was, according to Ian Watt, "widely held, not only by employers
and economic theorists, but by many of the poor themselves, both in the town and the country."[8] But the novel
itself did come in for a full share of adverse criticism. Relatively available—especially to domestic servants, despite the
high cost of books—and easy to read, it might present to the
poor a possible world glowing with luxury and social advantage; stirring their imaginations, it might arouse dissatisfaction with a life of poverty and privation and lead to
a desire to improve their material circumstances, with the
result that the social hierarchy would be in some danger of
upheaval. Such was the argument, benighted by humani-
tarian standards but plausible enough from the point of

view of anyone bred to the notion of class distinction. There was, of course, opposition to such an attitude; ironically, however, those who led the opposition were the very ones who would have religious scruples against fiction. Ultimately, in nineteenth-century England, hostility to fiction could take a utilitarian as well as an evangelical form. For Bentham, Kingsley, Froude, and Macaulay, poetry and fiction lacked truth and utility; for Carlyle, the association of fiction with Christian myth led to a disparaging of the imagination and an attempt to seek out a literature of fact (history) as the only valid basis for religious belief. A rigid distinction between history and fiction, between the actual and the possible, could thus come about for more than one reason. Mr. Houghton shows us that Victorian hostility to the imagination was part of a larger, more inclusive anti-intellectualism, typified by Samuel Smiles's observation in *Self-Help* (1859) that great and useful deeds do not depend on reading and writing, that the Magna Charta "was secured by men who signed the deed with their marks."[9]

A rigid social conservatism based on class awareness and a broad anti-intellectualism are thus historically affiliated with English opposition to the imagination; neither of these things has an exact counterpart in the American suspicion of the imagination. In both countries, fiction as an imaginative product was found to lack truth and utility; in the United States, however, the imagination was feared as a more immediate danger than in England (as if the Puritan strain conditioned anti-intellectualism more in America than it did in England)—the threat was felt to be greater because of the very lack of a history which would blend it with other concerns. Colonel Manly of Royall Tyler's *The Contrast* can be said to be anti-intellectual and implicitly anti-imaginative; even more accurately, however, one can say that he is suspicious of experience, that he demonstrates the relationship of ignorance to a certain kind of patriotism. Proudly he announces to the foppish Billy Dimple that he was "never ten leagues from the continent." When Dimple says that the "brilliant exhibitions of Europe" will lead Manly to despise the petty amusements of America, the Colonel replies: "Therefore I do not wish to see them; for I can never esteem that knowledge valuable, which tends to give me a distaste for my native country." He has read only a little—but enough to discover "a laudable partiality, which ignorant, untravelled men entertain for everything that belongs to their native country." Manly's suspicion of travel and refinement represents a certain head-in-the-sand patriotism that bears some similarity to Samuel Smiles's pride in the unlettered greatness of the signers of the Magna Charta. But Manly is defensively patriotic, whereas Smiles is proud of what he considers the most significant part of his heritage; to Manly, travel and sophistication form a distinct threat to the nation; to Smiles, learning is unnecessary to the great tradition, more obfuscating, finally, than threatening. Fear of the imagination in the United States seems, most distinctively, to have been allied to a suspicion of experience: Manly can be contrasted with Florio, the rake of William Hill Brown's *Ira and Isabella*, who, we recall, advocated living all the days of one's life, and with Dorcasina Sheldon, the ultimately pathetic heroine of *Female Quixotism*, who wastes her life trying to find the husband of her imagination. Florio courts experience, while Dorcasina dreams of it, but experience, actual or possible, constitutes a threat (to the national interest, in Manly's opinion) because it may breed dissatisfaction. Since imagination opens the way to vast new areas of experience, it is suspect. Manly, to his own satisfaction, has enough intelligence to know what he ought not to know. American anti-intellectualism, like that of England, is thus related to anti-imaginativeness, but the relation is, I think, reversed. In the United States, anti-intellectualism was part of a larger, more inclusive suspicion of the imagination (of, we may say, the possibilities of experience). The dangers of the imagination were not so historically defined as they were in England; consequently the threat was more immediate—it stood apart from class, party, and questions of authentic tradition as a danger in its own right. Precisely because nineteenth-century America was not nineteenth-century England, the imagination could be relatively isolated and feared as such.

In its largest implications, suspicion of the imagination is, of course, not restricted in time any more than in place. If today the novel has acquired a large degree of respectability, the battleground over the effects of imagination has been shifted to the various sub-literary forms that pervade modern culture (so that the suspicion of the imagination appears to be a human constant and the specific target for attack a cultural variable). Perennially, church groups and parent-teacher associations point out the danger of allowing children to maintain a steady reading diet of comic books; such warnings, as we know, are directed primarily against those anomalous productions of our culture called horror comics. Many other adults, individually, see a danger in allowing their children unrestricted access to these horror comics in which, it seems, fiendish monsters, now most likely from outer space, find it necessary to saw scantily-clad beautiful women in half with atomic saws in a mad quest to dominate the universe.[10] Objections to the sadism, to the violence and brutality of horror comics (and their pulp-magazine brethren) take essentially the same form as earlier objections to the novel. Such monstrous fabrications, we argue, strike through the imagination to warp one's sense of reality. Our terms of objection may differ from those used a century and a half ago; we now prefer to speak of "sickness" and "health" in an often disenchanting jargon; but it is the old story over again, in reality just as moral as ever: the imagination is still able to frighten the upholders of the social structure into protest. The imagination is still being accused of subversion. Indeed, in an attempt to give our children what might now be called proper reading experiences, we have even altered fairy tales and nursery rhymes (Miss Muffet might now share her curds and whey with an engaging spider), thus going a step beyond any suggestion made by Dr. James Gray, who prescribed fact and doctrine as adult fare, but who would allow ghosts, hobgoblins, and enchanted castles for children. The amusement we at times derive from the hyper-serious attention early Americans bestowed on novel-reading is thus ill-founded if it merely feeds our sense of superiority; if we must laugh at their seriousness, and at times we must, we should be honest enough to admit that we are also laughing at ourselves—as we would have been (and were) then, and as we are now.

That some contemporary criticism of imaginative excess is shrill, irresponsible, and undiscriminating does not permit us to evade or explain away our own problem. For now, as well as a century or a century and a half ago, the most intelligent and perceptive critics see a danger in misusing the imagination. Thomas Jefferson in 1818 felt that an insidious obstacle to "good education is the inordinate passion prevalent for novels, and the time lost in that reading that should be instructively employed." Novels, he goes on, infect the mind with a poison that destroys one's natural respect for "reason and fact, plain and unadorned." Then only "the figments of fancy" attract attention: "The result is a bloated imagination, sickly judgment, and disgust towards all the real businesses of life."[11] And Elizabeth Sewell in 1953 laments the lack of originality and the obsession with brutality that characterize most contemporary science fiction. Divorced from normal life, says Miss Sewell, such fiction is "also dangerous for the young"; it is linked with the problems of illiteracy and juvenile delinquency (which is our way of saying that it is an obstacle to "good education"). "A sense of mental inadequacy and a frustrated imagination are appallingly dangerous" in Miss Sewell's view, "and the consequences of both in self-assertion at the level of sex or violence are before our eyes."[12] To W. H. Auden, the imagination is

beyond good *and* evil, but it is only with the help of imagination that I can become good *or* evil. Without imagination I remain an innocent animal, unable to become anything but what I already am. In order to become what I should become, therefore, I have to put my imagination to work, to limit its playful activities, to imagining those possibilities which, for me, are both permissible and real; if I allow it to be the master and play exactly as it likes, then I shall remain in a dream-like state of imagining everything I might become, without getting around to ever becoming anything. But, once imagination has done its work for me to the degree that, with its help, I have become what I should become, imagination has a right to demand its freedom to play without any limitation, for there is no longer any danger that I shall take its play seriously.[13]

Miss Sewell and Mr. Auden are among our most effective advocates of genuine imaginative vitality (and I believe they well represent the vitality and intelligence of our Anglo-American tradition). Both see the imagination as integral to full participation in living. Yet both see it as capable of misuse and therefore as requiring control and direction. Miss Sewell considers the imagination to be a power, "half-spiritual, half-fleshly, essentially unitive and all-embracing, which operates by transforming the self into, and by means of, images of bodies, and perceiving or generating complexes of relations between its images which may bear analogy to other such complexes exterior to itself or apprehended in a different manner, as for instance by the intellect or the soul."[14] These are the "general conditions of imaginative processes," which can operate only in a given time and place. In our milieu, the misuse or quasi-use of the imagination leads Miss Sewell to issue warnings of grave social consequence. Mr. Auden posits a kind of moral imperative in his statement on the imagination: if it does what it *should* or *ought to* do, it wins the right to play. But, initially, the individual imagination contends with both valid and invalid possibilities, and the invalid possibilities constitute a serious danger. Not every imaginative possibility, that is, is a real possibility for a given person (and once again we see the tendency to wed morals and metaphysics). Mr. Auden offers the example of imagining himself to be a great heavyweight boxer as an essentially unreal and thus unpermissible (or, just as well in these terms, an essentially unpermissible and hence unreal) possibility for him. It could accomplish nothing for him; it would be futile and unproductive. Rightly used, then, the imagination has a responsibility to the actual world—possibility comes to serve actuality. The imagination must investigate the possible with the intention of leading us to actual achievement of some kind (if one is to become anything but what he already is). Having done this, it has won the right to play, for, as Mr. Auden says, "there is no longer any danger that I shall take its play seriously." The ability to see play as play is mandatory if one is to control and discipline the imagination properly.

What Jefferson calls a "bloated imagination" Mr. Auden terms an unrestricted, playful imagination; what Jefferson calls "sickly judgment" Miss Sewell terms "a sense of mental inadequacy"—the consequence, in both cases, of the aberrant imagination. For all three, the imagination poses a kind of threat because of its capacity to wean us from, in Jefferson's phrase, "the real business of life."

Society will always suspect the imagination as capable of subversion, I believe, in any time and place. Suspecting it, society will seek the most efficacious means of controlling it and putting it to work in some way in the cause of actuality. Despite the pervasive importance of idealisms, our implicit philosophical preference continues to give a metaphysical primacy to the actual order; existentialism tends to bring our moral attention to bear even more closely on actuality. We test our command of possibility by our ability to relate it to actuality. And the terms of social existence insist on such a command, for without it there is the potential danger of subversion.

My purpose in this study has been to examine an important means of controlling the imagination in the early United States and to suggest its effect on the beginnings of American fiction. The Puritan case against the imagination could not survive intact the dilution of Puritan theology; but with the Scottish philosophy of Common Sense in the service of apologetics, the old arguments could be given a new force; the imagination could be contained and controlled in a respectable, safe, and enlightened manner which would have important effects on the attempt to conceive and execute fiction. My investigations thus operate as prolegomena to a future study of American fiction in their attempt to enlarge our understanding of what it has been to write fiction in the United States; my hope is that they prepare us to know better the good and the bad fiction that we have. For as we understand more fully the conceptual context in which American fiction originated, we become better able to understand the fiction itself and the achievement it embodies.

As a force for stability in the early United States, and (from my point of view) as a means to control the American imagination, the Scottish philosophy of Common Sense held a position of authority and importance which dwindled, as we have seen, under the impact of transcendental thought. When Kant, Darwin, and Hegel became influential in the United States, few people studied Thomas Reid or Dugald Stewart. James McCosh at Princeton (from 1868 to 1888), it is true, perpetuated a Scottish tradition in American philosophy: "if there is to be an American philosophy," said McCosh, "it must be realistic"—it will not be idealistic. "The circumstance that Emerson is an American may seem to contradict this," he admits; "but then Emerson, while he opens interesting glimpses of truth, is not a philosopher; his thoughts are like strung pearls, without system and without connection."[15] McCosh proposed an extreme realism, suggesting that the "Scottish School must be made to throw away its crutches of impressions, instincts, suggestions, and common sense, and give the mind a power of seeing things directly"; only in this way can one attain "a true philosophy of reality."[16] Despite McCosh's articulateness, however, and the critical attention he gave to Common Sense thought, Scottish realism passed into a kind of philosophical limbo in the later nineteenth century. Writing in 1879, G. Stanley Hall notes that in the colleges the president was still "invariably" in charge of the senior-year courses in mental philosophy; unfortunately, he continues, trustees, "constituencies," and bequests frequently determine the nature of philosophical instruction, with the result that teachers of philosophy all too often lack initiative and independence. "Some of the professorlings of philosophy are disciples of disciples of Hopkins, Hickok, Wayland, Upham, Haven," he writes. "Most have extended their philosophical horizon as far as Reid, Stewart, Hamilton." Many have gone on to

Mill, Spencer, Huxley, Kant, Berkeley, Hegel, and Hume. Some are attempting essays of their own; and a few are doing valuable and original work.[17] Through occasional strokes of mild satire we may see the essential drift of Hall's argument, which I take to be typical of the time. For genuine philosophical achievement, he is saying, one must move away from or past the Scots. Outside the colleges such a movement was definitely taking place. Hall finds the primary philosophical influence to be that of Hegel ("represented, since 1867," by William T. Harris' *Journal of Speculative Philosophy*) and of Herbert Spencer ("greatly extended" by E. L. Youman's *Popular Science Monthly*).[18] But other men were becoming known as well, so that, as Hall sees it, "the most general characteristic of American intellectual life is its homogeneity."[19] This he commends, singling out for special comment the work of a new philosopher who promises to be extremely important, Charles Sanders Peirce.

Though Scottish Common Sense thought came to be considered a naive and old-fashioned mode of philosophical inquiry, we may note—in fairness to the Scots—that Peirce, one of the toughest-minded and most independent of American thinkers, not only knew their work but built on it with modification. Peirce defines common sense as "the resultant of the traditional experience of mankind, [which] witnesses unequivocally that the heart is more than the head"—an interesting statement when one thinks of Hawthorne's belief in the heart and suspicion of the head.[20] As part of his pragmaticism, Peirce formulates a Critical Common-Sensism which differs in four basic ways from the Common Sense philosophy of the "old Scotch School." He holds "that all the veritably indubitable beliefs are vague—often in some directions highly so"; he takes "a modern" view of evolution, perceiving that we can outgrow the applicability of instinct as we develop degrees of self-control; he has "a high esteem for doubt"; and, finally, he "criticizes the critical method, follows its footsteps, tracks it to its lair."[21] "A pure Kantist" until (as he says) he became a pragmaticist, Peirce recognizes the achievement of the Scottish philosophers as limited in method, and conditioned by its context of belief and opinion, but nonetheless worth adapting for his purposes. In the matter of common sense, he owns his "adherence, under inevitable modification, to the opinion of that subtle but well-balanced intellect, Thomas Reid."[22] With all the modifications taken into account, Peirce's Critical Common-Sensism owes an acknowledged debt to "the famous Scotch philosophers" and demonstrates the durability of their central position.

And Peirce, too, comments on the imagination in a manner by now familiar to us. In his case, as we might expect, it is the scientific imagination, but the terms of his statement are essentially those of Mr. Auden, Dr. James Gray, and numerous other critics whose opinions we have encountered. "When a man desires ardently to know the truth," says Peirce, "his first effort will be to imagine what that truth may be." But one "cannot prosecute his pursuit long without finding that imagination unbridled is sure to carry him off the track." Though no "inkling of the truth" will come to the scientist without imagination, "mere dreaming of opportunities for gain" (and "mere artistic imagination") are of no value to him: "The scientific imagination dreams of explanations and laws."[23] Control is again the imperative; the imagination is necessary, but is capable of subverting inquiry.

The "imagination unbridled is sure to carry him off the track": that refrain, running, as we have seen, from philosopher to poet to critic to scientist, constituted the essential warning against the imagination given to the citizens of the young American republic. That they would take it seriously and that it would have an effect on their attempts to produce fiction I have tried to demonstrate. Elsewhere Peirce says that "every man of us has a metaphysics, and has to have one; and it will influence his life greatly."[24] The implications of this statement bear directly on the subject at hand. In the first half of the nineteenth century, we may say, American society had a predominantly Common Sense metaphysics which pervaded theological, moral, and social concerns to influence greatly the conceptual and creative life of the period. As a metaphysics of assurance, it helped to resolve the issues of consolidation; as a metaphysics of actuality, it helped to shape the course of American fiction.

NOTES

Chapter One

1. G. Stanley Hall, "On the History of American College Textbooks and Teaching in Logic, Ethics, Psychology and Allied Subjects," *Proceedings of the American Antiquarian Society*, n. s., IX (1893–94), 158.

2. I. Woodbridge Riley, *American Thought from Puritanism to Pragmatism and Beyond* (New York, 1915), p. 135. Merle Curti, *The Growth of American Thought* (New York, 1943), p. 236. Roy Harvey Pearce, *The Savages of America: A Study of the Indian and the Idea of Civilization* (Baltimore, 1953), pp. 88–89. Herbert W. Schneider, *A History of American Philosophy* (New York, 1946), p. 249.

3. Schneider, *Philosophy*, pp. 247–48.

4. Frederick Beasley, *A Search for Truth in the Science of the Human Mind*, Part I (Philadelphia, 1822), pp. ii–iii. An interesting account of John Witherspoon at Princeton can be found in James McCosh, *John Witherspoon and His Times* (Philadelphia, 1890), pp. 21ff. McCosh has been perhaps the chief exponent of philosophical realism in America; he believed that realism was the American philosophy. Accordingly, he says that Witherspoon introduced the "wholesome philosophy" of Common Sense at Princeton, "where it has ever since been taught—I hope with some improvements to make it more consistently realistic—down to the present day" (p. 22). Varnum L. Collins, *President Witherspoon: A Biography* (Princeton, 1925), supersedes the earlier biography, *John Witherspoon* (1906), by David W. Woods. *The Lives of Eighteen from Princeton*, ed. Willard Thorp (Princeton, 1946), has valuable essays on eminent Princetonians, and Thomas J. Wertenbaker,

Princeton: 1746–1896 (Princeton, 1946), contains an excellent treatment of the early college. In *American Thought. . .* , pp. 126–30, I. Woodbridge Riley has a concise account of the philosophical implications of Witherspoon's arrival at Princeton.

5. Samuel Miller, *A Brief Retrospect of the Eighteenth Century,* 2 vols. (New York, 1803), II, 376–77. See also *John Witherspoon Comes to America,* ed. Lyman H. Butterfield (Princeton, 1953).

6. *The Autobiography of Benjamin Rush,* ed. George W. Corner (Princeton, 1948), p. 51.

7. The lectures were later published: *Lectures on Moral Philosophy and Eloquence,* 3rd ed. (Philadelphia, 1810). A corrected edition, entitled *Lectures on Moral Philosophy* (Philadelphia, 1822), included "An Address to the Students of the Senior Class" of 1775 and "Letters on Education and Marriage." In *The Quest for Nationality* (Syracuse, N. Y., 1957), Benjamin T. Spencer points out that Witherspoon's lectures clarified some of the implications of Common Sense thought for an American style (p. 11).

8. McCosh believes that "few teachers in the world's history have left behind so many eminent pupils who engaged in great and noble work" (*Witherspoon and His Times,* p. 28). My partial enumeration is drawn from John Maclean, *History of the College of New Jersey, from its Origin in 1746 to the Commencement of 1854,* 2 vols. (Philadelphia, 1877), I, 357–62. Maclean's *History* is still valuable for the information it contains in bulk. He includes a much more extensive list of graduates under Witherspoon's administration who achieved illustrious later careers.

9. Adrienne Koch, *The Philosophy of Thomas Jefferson* (New York, 1943), pp. 17–18. Jefferson owned Kames's *Essays on the Principles of Morality and Natural Religion* (Edinburgh, 1751) and *Introduction to the Art of Thinking,* 2nd ed. (Edinburgh, 1764). See *Catalogue of the Library of Thomas Jefferson,* compiled and annotated by E. Millicent Sowerby, 2 vols. (Washington, D. C., 1953).

10. *The Commonplace Book of Thomas Jefferson: A Repertory of His Ideas on Government,* ed. Gilbert Chinard (Baltimore, 1926), pp. 16–19.

11. Pearce, *Savages,* pp. 94–96.

12. *The Writings of Thomas Jefferson,* ed. Albert Ellery Bergh (Washington, D. C., 1907), XIV, 144, letter to Thomas Law, June 13, 1814. Eleanor Davidson Berman illustrates Jefferson's large esthetic indebtedness to Kames in *Thomas Jefferson Among the*

Arts (New York, 1947) and mentions Thomas Reid as one "who provided the climate of intellectual opinion within which Jefferson's own views took shape" (p. 34).

13. *Writings of Jefferson*, XV, 239–40, letter to John Adams, March 14, 1820.

14. Gilbert Chinard, *Jefferson et les Idéologues* (Baltimore and Paris, 1925), p. 1.

15. *Writings of Jefferson*, XVIII, 331, letter to Dugald Stewart, April 26, 1824. *Elements of the Philosophy of the Human Mind* was printed at Philadelphia in 1793, at Brattleboro, Vermont, in 1808 and again in 1813, and on three other occasions in the United States up to 1864. Other American printings of Stewart's works include *Philosophical Essays* (New York, 1811); *A General View of the Progress of Metaphysical, Ethical, and Political Philosophy, Since the Revival of Letters in Europe* (Boston, 1817 and 1822); *The Philosophy of the Active and Moral Powers of Man* (Boston, 1828), which went through nine American editions to 1866; and the *Works of Dugald Stewart*, 7 vols. (Cambridge, [Mass.], 1829).

16. *Autobiography of Rush*, p. 150.

17. Ibid., p. 110, fn. by George W. Corner.

18. Charles Page Smith, *James Wilson, Founding Father, 1742–1798* (Chapel Hill, 1956), p. 341.

19. Ibid., pp. 321, 333.

20. A. F. Tytler (Lord Woodhouselee), *Memoirs of the Life and Writings of the Honourable Henry Home of Kames*, 2 vols. (Edinburgh and London, 1807), I, 263.

21. Ibid., I, 269.

22. Ibid., pp. 262–63.

23. Ibid., II, 10–11, 21. The versatility of the careers of Kames and Franklin suggests certain parallels in their lives. Franklin notes this in a letter of February 21, 1769 in which he congratulates Kames on his election as President of the Edinburgh Society. "I think I formerly took notice to you in conversation," he writes, "that I thought there had been some similarity in our fortunes, and the circumstances of our lives. This is a fresh instance, for, by letters just received, I find that I was about the same time chosen President of our American Philosophical Society, established at Philadelphia" (ibid., p. 86).

24. See Koch, *Philosophy of Jefferson*, Chap. VI, "Philosophical Debut," pp. 44–53.

25. Gentz's essay, translated by John Quincy Adams, is conven-

iently available in a paperback edition: *The French and American Revolutions Compared* (Chicago, Gateway Edition, 1955). My quotation is from page 47 of this edition.

26. Alexis de Tocqueville, *Democracy in America*, 2 vols. (Vintage Edition, 1954), II, 232–35; II, 202; II, 108.

27. Clinton Rossiter, *Conservatism in America* (New York, 1955), pp. 17, 53. Charles McClean Andrews examines "Conservative Factors in Early Colonial History," *Authority and the Individual* (Cambridge, [Mass.], 1937), pp. 154–69.

28. Paul R. Anderson and Max H. Fisch, *Philosophy in America* (New York, 1939), p. 297. Anderson and Fisch give a lucid exposition of Smith's ideas.

29. William H. Hudnutt, III, "Samuel Stanhope Smith: Enlightened Conservative," *Journal of the History of Ideas*, XVII (1956), 542; an excellent treatment of Smith as President of Princeton. Smith hired as Professor of Natural Philosophy and Mathematics the Scottish chemist John Maclean, who became "the first undergraduate teacher of chemistry and natural science in the United States" (p. 541).

30. Samuel Stanhope Smith, *An Essay on the Variety of Complexion and Figure in the Human Species. . .* [and] *Strictures on Lord Kaim's Discourse on the Original Diversity of Mankind* (Philadelphia, 1787).

31. Hudnutt, "Smith," p. 544.

32. *The American Quarterly Review*, I (1827), 17.

33. Samuel Stanhope Smith, *The Lectures, Corrected and Improved, which Have Been Delivered for a Series of Years in the College of New Jersey; on the Subjects of Moral and Political Philosophy*, 2 vols. (Trenton, N. J., 1812), I, 20.

34. Ibid., p. 139.

35. Sidney Willard, *Memories of Youth and Manhood*, 2 vols. (Cambridge, [Mass.], 1855), I, 269–70.

36. William Charvat, *The Origins of American Critical Thought, 1810–1835* (Philadelphia, 1936), p. 32. See Charvat's sketch of E. T. Channing, *Origins*, pp. 185–87. Channing's lectures were published as *Lectures Read to the Seniors in Harvard College* (Boston, 1856).

37. Levi Hedge, *A Treatise on the Philosophy of the Human Mind, being the Lectures of the Late Thomas Brown, M. D. . . . Abridged and Distributed according to the natural divisions of the subject* (Cambridge, [Mass.], 1827), Preface, pp. iii–v.

38. Edgeley W. Todd, "Philosophical Ideas at Harvard College, 1817–1837," *New England Quarterly*, XVI (1943), 65.

39. *North American Review*, IV (1817), 86.

40. The document drawn up by the executors of Alford's estate for the establishment of the Alford Professorship is printed in Levi Frisbie's *Inaugural Address, Delivered in the Chapel of the University at Cambridge, November 5, 1817* (Cambridge, [Mass.], 1817), pp. 4–7. The most pertinent section states that the "principal duty" of the incumbent shall be "to demonstrate the existence of a Deity or first cause, to prove and illustrate his essential attributes, both natural and moral; to evince and explain his providence and government, together with the doctrine of a future state of rewards and punishments; also to deduce and enforce the obligations which man is under to his Maker, and the duties which he owes him, resulting from the perfections of the Deity, and from his own rational nature, together with the most important duties of social life, resulting from the several relations which men mutually bear to each other; and likewise the several duties which respect ourselves, founded not only in our own interest but also in the will of God; interspersing the whole with remarks, shewing the coincidence between the doctrines of revelation and the dictates of reason in these important points; and lastly, notwithstanding this coincidence, to state the absolute necessity and vast utility of a divine revelation.

"He shall also read a distinct course of lectures upon that branch of Moral Philosophy, which respects the application of the law of nature to nations, and their relative rights and duties: and also on the absolute necessity of civil government in some form, and the reciprocal rights and duties of magistrates and of the people resulting from the social impact; and also on the various forms of government, which have existed or may exist in the world, pointing out their respective advantages and disadvantages, and what form of government is best adapted to promote the greatest happiness of mankind."

41. Benjamin Rand, "Philosophical Instruction in Harvard University from 1636 to 1900," *Harvard Graduates Magazine*, XXXVIII (1928–29), 189–95. Rand and Edgeley W. Todd, "Philosophical Ideas," give specific information about textbooks used at Harvard. The *North American Review* in 1818 carried a "Circular Letter relating to Harvard University," which gave a list of required courses, textbooks, and "private exercises" (VI [1818], 421–30).

42. Francis Bowen, "Locke and the Transcendentalists," *The Christian Examiner and General Review*, XXIII (1838), 170.

43. Merle Curti, "The Great Mr. Locke, America's Philosopher, 1783–1861," *The Huntington Library Bulletin*, No. 11 (1937), 107–51.

44. *North American Review*, XII (1821), 396. Gilman is here referring to Richard François Phillipe Brunck (1729–1803), French classical scholar, who published numerous editions of the Greek classics, and Marie Joseph de Gerando (1772–1842), French philosopher, whose best known work is *Histoire comparée des systèmes de philosophie relativement aux principes des connaissances humaines,* 3 vols. (Paris, 1804).

45. Rand, "Philosophical Instruction," p. 46. See also Leon Howard, *Victorian Knight-Errant: A Study of the Early Literary Career of James Russell Lowell* (Berkeley and Los Angeles, 1952), p. 15.

46. Leon Howard, *The Connecticut Wits* (Chicago, 1943), p. 12.

47. Ibid., p. 11.

48. Ibid., p. 26.

49. Louis Franklin Snow, *The College Curriculum in the United States* (New York, 1907), p. 129, n.

50. *Quarterly Register and Journal of the American Education Society,* I (1829), 231.

51. Sydney E. Ahlstrom, "The Scottish Philosophy and American Theology," *Church History*, XXIV (1955), 267.

52. Ibid., pp. 262–65. Ahlstrom quotes Park to the effect that " 'New England divinity has been marked by a strong, practical common sense. Our later theologians. . . were adepts in the philosophy of Reid, Oswald, Campbell, Beattie, Stewart; and this has been termed the philosophy of common sense' " (p. 265).

53. Ibid., p. 268.

54. For a thorough treatment of Scottish emigration and colonization in North America, see Ian Charles Cargill Graham, *Colonists from Scotland: Emigration to North America, 1707–1783* (Ithaca, N. Y., 1956). See also Whitfield J. Bell, Jr., "Scottish Emigration to America: A Letter of Dr. Charles Nisbet to Dr. John Witherspoon, 1784," *The William and Mary Quarterly*, XI (1954), 276–89. This April, 1954 number of *The William and Mary Quarterly* is devoted to "Scotland and America."

55. Wright discusses colleges, books, periodicals, and libraries in

the West in his *Culture on the Moving Frontier* (Bloomington, Indiana, 1955). See especially Chaps. II and III.

56. George P. Schmidt, *The Old Time College President* (New York and London, 1930), p. 27.

57. Ibid., p. 96.

58. *The American Quarterly Register*, IV (1831), 13–14.

59. Frederick W. Seward, *Reminiscences of a War-time Statesman and Diplomat* (New York, 1916), p. 65.

60. *Autobiography of Rush*, p. 267.

61. Robert Samuel Fletcher, *A History of Oberlin College From Its Foundation Through the Civil War*, 2 vols. (Oberlin, Ohio, 1943), II, 701–2.

62. See Chap. IV, "The Bearer of the Old Tradition," pp. 108–45. In chapters two and three Schmidt gives us our most thorough sketch of the college president before 1860, his duties, functions, and place in the world. Wilson Smith, *Professors and Public Ethics* (Ithaca, N. Y., 1956), examines "The Pattern of Moral Philosophy" (pp. 28–43) and stresses the public function of the moral philosopher (pp. 3–27). Smith warns against overestimating the influence of Common Sense philosophy in the decades prior to the Civil War, though he admits that the "almost phenomenal sales" of Francis Wayland's *The Elements of Moral Science* seem to indicate that Common Sense "was the dominant philosophy taught to college students" (p. 29, n.).

63. Schmidt, *President*, p. 128.

64. Ibid., pp. 109–10.

65. Wilson Smith, *Professors*, p. 3. Alfred Zantzinger Reed, *Training for the Public Profession of the Law* (New York, 1921), deals with the moral philosophy course as part of legal training. See Anne Haddow, *Political Science in American Colleges and Universities, 1636–1900* (New York, 1939), Chap. V, "Political Science as a Part of Moral Philosophy, 1770–1825," for an examination of the topic suggested by the chapter title. Herbert A. Adams, *The Study of History in American Colleges and Universities* (Washington, D.C., 1887), finds that professors of moral philosophy could include history in their province. Citing the case of Francis Bowen at Harvard who taught and wrote history, Adams emphasizes the "mosaic character" of the moral philosopher's work (pp. 23–24).

66. Schmidt, *President*, p. 143.

67. See the partial list of "Senior Studies" in the *Quarterly Register and Journal of the American Education Society*, I (1829), 232.

68. Charvat, *Origins*, pp. 30–31. The Andover Seminary Library "owned many copies of all the Scotch philosophers' works, including an edition of Brown published at Andover in 1822"; in 1828 Andover adopted Thomas Brown into its curriculum (pp. 34–35).

69. Spencer, *Quest*, pp. 33–34.

70. *Elements of Criticism*, ed. Rev. James R. Boyd (New York, 1868), pp. 3–4.

71. Ibid., p. 71.

72. Schneider, *American Philosophy*, pp. 254–56, gives "a chronological listing of the chief texts concerning both mental and moral philosophy" from 1822 to 1892. His list comprises forty-five titles. G. Stanley Hall appends to his article "American College Textbooks" a long list of books used as texts in logic, ethics, and psychology in American colleges (pp. 162–74); the works of the Scottish Common Sense philosophers as well as American abridgements of these works are heavily represented.

73. William G. Roelker, "Francis Wayland: A Neglected Pioneer of Higher Education," *Proceedings of the American Antiquarian Society*, LIII (1943), 42.

74. Ezra Stiles Ely, *Conversations on the Science of the Human Mind* (Philadelphia, 1819), Preface, p. v.

75. Ibid., p. 14.

76. Ibid., p. 20.

77. Miller, *Brief Retrospect*, II, 10–12.

78. George Gates Raddin, Jr. has made a series of studies of Caritat and the early city of New York: *An Early New York Library of Fiction* (New York, 1940); *Hocquet Caritat and the Early New York Literary Scene* (Dover, N. J., 1953); *Caritat and the Genet Episode* (Dover, N. J., 1953); and *The New York of Hocquet Caritat and His Associates, 1797–1817* (Dover, N. J., 1953). Raddin cites the passage referring to Stewart in *An Early New York Library of Fiction*, p. 14.

79. *Monthly Anthology and Boston Review*, IV (1808), 364.

80. Marjorie H. Nicholson discusses Marsh's contribution to American transcendental thought in "James Marsh and the Vermont Transcendentalists," *Philosophical Review*, XXXIV (1925), 28–48. See also John Dewey, "James Marsh and American Philosophy," *Journal of the History of Ideas*, II (1941), 131–50 and Lewis

S. Feuer, "James Marsh and the Conservative Transcendentalist Philosophy: A Political Interpretation," *New England Quarterly*, XXXI (1958), 3–31.

81. *The Remains of the Rev. James Marsh, D. D.*, edited, with a "Memoir," by J. L. Torrey (Boston, 1843), p. 136.

82. Thomas Cooper, "Outline of the Association of Ideas," in his translation of F. J. V. Broussais, *On Irritation and Insanity: to which are Added two Tracts on Materialism and an Outline of the Association of Ideas* (Columbia, S. C., 1831), p. 380. The tracts are "The Scripture Doctrine of Materialism" and "A View of the Metaphysical and Physiological Arguments in Favor of Materialism," both of which were published anonymously in Philadelphia in 1823.

83. The Farmer's Library is now part of the special collections of the University of Rochester Library. I am indebted to Professor Philip B. Daghlian of Indiana University for telling me of the Library and for allowing me to use his photostatic records of its holdings.

84. William P. Hudson, "Archibald Alison and William Cullen Bryant," *American Literature*, XII (1940), 60.

85. Merrell R. Davis, "Emerson's 'Reason' and the Scottish Philosophers," *New England Quarterly*, XVII (1944), 215–17.

86. Emerson's "Dissertation" is available in *Two Unpublished Essays. . . by Ralph Waldo Emerson*, ed. Edward E. Hale (Boston, 1896). My quotation is from pp. 68–69.

87. Ibid., p. 76. Leon Howard illustrates "how readily the doctrines of Emerson soared out of the principles of Dugald Stewart," *Victorian Knight-Errant*, pp. 17–18.

88. Ralph L. Rusk, *The Life of Ralph Waldo Emerson* (New York, 1949), p. 91.

89. Edward Waldo Emerson, *Emerson in Concord: A Memoir* (Boston, 1890), p. 31.

90. *The Letters of Ralph Waldo Emerson*, ed. Ralph L. Rusk, 6 vols. (New York, 1939), I, 125, Nov. 25, 1822. Emerson is apparently referring to Stewart's *A General View of the Progress of Metaphysical, Ethical, and Political Philosophy, since the Revival of Letters in Europe* (Boston, 1822). On his twenty-sixth birthday in 1795, the Rev. William Emerson, Ralph's father, had been reading the author who in a sense was the intellectual father of Dugald Stewart. He wrote in his journal for that day: "Planted my watermelons and musk melons. Wrote two prayers. Attended and prayed

in town-meeting. Came home and read Tho. Reid's intellectual powers, which is now my *author* on hand." See Rusk, *Life of Emerson*, p. 3; William Emerson refers to Thomas Reid's *Essays on the Intellectual Powers of Man.*

91. In "Thoreau's Philosophical Apprenticeship," *New England Quarterly*, XVIII (1945), 51-69, James Kwiat points out (pp. 51-53) that Francis Bowen "showed a wide familiarity with the Scottish school in his essays appearing in the *Christian Examiner* and the *North American Review*, which were collected under the title *Critical Essays*, in 1842. He revised and abridged, with critical and explanatory notes for the use of colleges, Stewart's *Elements of the Philosophy of the Human Mind* in 1854."

92. Ibid., p. 60.

93. Ibid., pp. 65-67. Thoreau's library contained an 1822 abridgement of Blair's *Lectures on Rhetoric*, two editions of Blair's *Sermons* (Philadelphia, 1794; and 2 vols., Boston, 1799), and Stewart's *Elements of the Philosophy of the Human Mind*, 2 vols. (Cambridge, 1833). See Walter Harding, *Thoreau's Library* (Charlottesville, Va., 1957).

94. Howard, *Victorian Knight-Errant*, p. 23. Lowell's father, the Rev. Dr. Charles Lowell, had studied in Edinburgh, "where he received personal attentions and particular kindnesses from Dugald Stewart" (ibid., p. 6).

95. Ibid., see pp. 342-46.

96. "The Convert; or, Leaves from My Experience," *The Works of Orestes A. Brownson*, 20 vols. (Detroit, 1882-87), V, 124. Pierre Leroux's *Réfutation de l' Éclectisme* (1839) later had the "marvellous effect" of "emancipating" Brownson from his "subjection to the eclectic school founded by Cousin and Jouffroy." The work of Jouffroy was significantly influenced by Reid and Stewart, while, as an apostle of eclecticism, Cousin was well acquainted with the principles of Common Sense thought.

97. Thomas Brown, *Lectures on the Philosophy of the Human Mind*, 15th ed. (Edinburgh, 1845), pp. 35-36. Dugald Stewart told Brown that he had received "*much* pleasure and *much* instruction" from an early version of the *Inquiry into the Relation of Cause and Effect* (ibid., p. x).

98. Brownson, "Philosophy and Common Sense," *Works*, I, 6-7, 18.

99. Ibid., p. 31.

100. Ibid., p. 386. Brownson has, however, a low opinion of Locke, whom he feels to be an easy, popular writer with practically nothing of importance to say (I, 11).

101. Ibid., pp. 397, 390.

102. Charvat, *Origins*, pp. 1–2.

103. *The Works of Thomas Reid, D. D.*, ed. Sir William Hamilton, 2 vols. (Edinburgh, 1853), I, 421.

104. "We notice with particular pleasure," he continues, "the sentence of just indignation, which the Edinburgh tribunal has pronounced upon Moore, Swift, Goethe, and in general the German sentimentalists." *Inaugural Address*, pp. 24–25.

105. Charvat, *Origins*, pp. 180–82; see also *William Hickling Prescott: Representative Selections*, ed. William Charvat and Michael Kraus, American Writers Series (New York, 1943), Introduction, pp. lxxix, xc–xci.

106. *American Review of History and Politics*, I (1811), 355.

107. Charvat, *Origins*, p. 172.

108. Robert Walsh, *Didactics: Social, Literary, and Political*, 2 vols. (Philadelphia, 1836), II, 251–52. Dr. Philip Tidyman of South Carolina purchased the portrait "at a cost of nearly five hundred dollars," presented it to the Pennsylvania Academy of Fine Arts, and engaged Thomas Sully (1783–1872), "who is in the first rank of American painters," to make a copy. Walsh quotes a portion of a letter from Stewart's wife to Dr. Tidyman concerning the portrait: " 'We are reproached for letting it go to America; but, in truth, it can no where be better bestowed. Besides regard for the friendship of the individual to whom it goes, America herself has, from Mr. Stewart's earliest years, possessed his deepest interest and anxious affection. None of her own sons can rejoice more sincerely in her prosperity, and it would be strange indeed if he were not highly gratified with the attention which his works have received in that country.' "

109. *North American Review*, XII (1821), 395.

110. *Christian Examiner*, IX (1830), 304.

111. Robert E. Streeter, "Association Psychology and Literary Nationalism in the *North American Review*, 1815–1825," *American Literature*, XVII (1945), 246. See also Martin Kallich, "The Association of Ideas and Critical Theory: Hobbes, Locke, and Addison," *ELH*, XII (1945), 315.

112. *North American Review*, XXIX (1829), 93–97.

113. Ibid., pp. 98–99.

114. Ibid., p. 100. In 1821, we recall, Samuel Gilman had said that Brown was "scarcely known in this country."

115. Ibid., p. 102. For Everett and the "back to Locke" movement, see Curti, "Mr. Locke," p. 130.

116. *The American Review*, II (1845), 390. This periodical was later called *The American Whig Review*.

117. Ibid., p. 391.

118. Ibid., p. 397.

119. *North American Review*, VI (1818), 224.

120. Ibid., p. 225 (Frisbie, *Inaugural Address*, p. 11).

121. Ibid., p. 226 (Frisbie, pp. 11–12).

122. Ibid., p. 230 (Frisbie, p. 24).

123. Henry Wheaton, *An Address, Pronounced at the Opening of the New-York Athenaeum, December 14, 1824* (New York, 1824), pp. 39, 43.

124. Ibid., p. 237 (Frisbie, pp. 26–27). In his essay "Progress and Perfectibility in Samuel Miller's Intellectual History," *Studies in Intellectual History* (Baltimore, 1953), Gilbert Chinard notes the distinction between the ideas of progress and perfectibility made by Miller in his *Brief Retrospect*. Chinard comments: "Whether the distinction established by Samuel Miller. . . was observed by many of his American contemporaries, I am not prepared to say" (p. 119). Levi Frisbie certainly made the same distinction, as did the reviewer of his address.

125. Ibid., pp. 237–38.

126. I have attempted to show this to be true of the American attitude toward the nation as reflected in early American fiction in "Social Institutions in the Early American Novel," *American Quarterly*, IX (1957), 75–76.

127. See R. W. B. Lewis, *The American Adam* (Chicago, 1955), for an examination into the nature and meaning of the American idea of being emancipated from history.

128. On the Scots and their supposed primitivism, see Donald M. Foerster, "Scottish Primitivism and the Historical Approach," *Philological Quarterly*, XXIX (1950), 307–323, and three items by Roy Harvey Pearce: "The Eighteenth-Century Scottish Primitivists: Some Reconsiderations," *ELH*, XII (1945), 203–20; his introduction to John Robert Scott, *Dissertation on the Progress of the Fine Arts*, The Augustan Reprint Society, No. 45 (1954), pp. i–viii; and,

more specifically relating to America, pp. 82-100 of *The Savages of America*.

129. *North American Review*, VI (1818), 239-41.

130. Ibid., p. 241. Statements of a similar belief in the American future can be found in such places as John Bristed, *An Oration on the Utility of Literary Establishments*. . . (New York, 1814), p. 7, and John Frederick Schroeder, D. D., *The Intellectual and Moral Resources of Horticulture: An Anniversary Discourse, Pronounced before the New-York Horticultural Society, at the Annual Celebration*. . ., 3rd ed. (New York, 1838), p. 16. See also Wheaton, *Address*, p. 43. From the beginning, Americans have talked much, and eloquently, of their future.

Chapter Two

1. See Herbert Ross Brown, *The Sentimental Novel in America, 1789-1810* (Durham, N.C., 1940), especially Chapters One and Two; G. Harrison Orians, "Censure of Fiction in American Romances and Magazines, 1789-1810," *PMLA*, LII (1937), 195-214; and Ormond E. Palmer, "Some Attitudes Toward Fiction in America to 1870, and a Bit Beyond" (unpublished dissertation, University of Chicago, 1952), especially Chapters Three and Four.

Similar criticism of the novel existed, as we know, in England. Rather than repeat this fact each time I draw a conclusion about the American criticism, however, I have postponed my comparative comments until Chapter Four.

2. For a discussion of the antiromance motif of the novel as formulated by Cervantes, see Harry Levin, "The Example of Cervantes," in *Society and Self in the Novel*, English Institute Essays (New York, 1956), pp. 23-24.

3. *The Port Folio*, n.s. [Series III], III (1807), 234. The Rev. Samuel Jarvis was perhaps better known to some of his contemporaries because of the divorce action brought against him by his wife, Sarah McCurdy Hart Jarvis, in 1839. See *The Great Divorce Case! A Full and Impartial History of the Trial of the Petition of Mrs. Sarah M. Jarvis, for a Divorce from Her Husband, the Rev. Samuel F. Jarvis, D. D., L. L. D., before a Committee of the Legislature of the State of Connecticut* (New York, 1839) and the *Report of the Proceedings, on the Petition of Mrs. Sarah M. Jarvis, for a . Divorce from her Husband, Rev. Samuel F. Jarvis, D. D., L. L. D.*,

before a Committee of the Legislature of Connecticut (Hartford, 1839).

4. For an interesting recent discussion of the manner in which the imagination confronts and deals with particularity (the finite), see William F. Lynch, S.J., "The Imagination and the Finite," *Thought*, XXXIII (1958), 205–28. Concerned with a theory of the imagination, Father Lynch does not of course seek to denigrate its operations. But he and Jarvis would agree that the imagination perforce must function with the finite; the crucial difference in their subsequent positions would be that for Jarvis the finite and the infinite are split apart absolutely and irreconcilably, while for Father Lynch the imagination, by analogy, seeks at its best for transcendence in and through particularity—for the analogical relationship between the finite and the infinite. I make a point of their agreement to emphasize the intellectual quality of Jarvis' attack on the novel; he saw then what we see now; and his auditors could justly consider themselves to be listening to an enlightened, thoughtful, and persuasive discourse, just as Father Lynch's readers can consider themselves to be in touch with a stimulating and excellent analysis. Father Lynch's analyses into the nature of the literary imagination are seen more fully in *Christ and Apollo: The Dimensions of the Literary Imagination* (New York, 1960).

5. Rev. William Jones, *Letters from a Tutor to His Pupils* (Oxford, 1841), p. 57.

6. See William B. Sprague, *Annals of the American Pulpit, or, Commemorative Notices of Distinguished American Clergymen of Various Denominations, from the Early Settlement of the Country to the Close of the Year 1855*, IX (New York, 1869), Part I, p. 97. Thomas Reid held his Professorship at Glasgow until his death in 1796.

7. Ibid., p. 95.

8. *The Port Folio*, n. s. [Series III], IV (1810), 94–97.

9. See Roy Harvey Pearce, "The Eighteenth-Century Scottish Primitivists: Some Reconsiderations," *ELH*, XII (1945), 203–20, for a discussion of Scottish primitivism and anti-primitivism.

10. James Beattie, *Dissertations Moral and Critical*, 2 vols. (Dublin, 1783), II, 320.

11. Crane Brinton, *Ideas and Men* (New York, 1950), pp. 19, 21.

12. Samuel Miller, *Brief Retrospect of the Eighteenth Century*, 2 vols. (New York, 1803), II, 174.

13. Ibid., pp. 176–79.

14. Ibid., p. 179, n.

15. *The Port Folio*, n. s. [Series III], III (1807), 209.

16. [Mrs. Martha Read], *Monima; or, the Beggar Girl* (New York, 1802), Preface, and *Monima*. . . (Philadelphia, 1803), p. iii.

17. Mrs. P. D. Manvill, *Lucinda; or, the Mountain Mourner* (Ithaca, 1839), pp. iii–iv. Beneath this testimonial are the names of Elias Gilbert, Minister of the Gospel, Greenfield; Mark A. Child, Esq., Greenfield; Ezra Nash, Justice of the Peace; E. White, Jun., Merchant, Ballston Spa; Asa C. Barney, M.D., Greenfield; Charles Deake, Deacon. . . , Greenfield; Lemuel Smith, Min. of the Gospel, Canajoharie; and the names of four members of the Society of Friends.

18. [Sukey Vickery], *Emily Hamilton* (Worcester, 1803), pp. 3–5.

19. *The Posthumous Works of Ann Eliza Bleecker, in Prose and Verse* (New York, 1793), p. 19.

20. [Hannah Webster Foster], *The Boarding School; or, Lessons of a Preceptress to Her Pupils* (Boston, 1829), pp. 16–17.

21. Herbert Ross Brown sees Mrs. Foster's claim of a factual foundation for her novel as "more than a conventional gesture designed to forestall the criticism of a generation of readers who had been taught to regard all fiction as lies." *The Coquette; or, the History of Eliza Wharton*, Facsimile Text Edition (New York, 1939), Introduction, p. x.

22. [William Hill Brown], *The Power of Sympathy*, 2 vols., Facsimile Text Edition (New York, 1937), I, 50.

23. *Coquette*, Facsimile Text Edition, Introduction, pp. xi–xii.

24. The quotation is from a letter from Reid to Dr. James Gregory, cited by Dugald Stewart, "Progress of Metaphysical and Ethical Philosophy," in *Dissertations on the History of Metaphysical and Ethical. . . Science* (Edinburgh, 1835), p. 218. Stewart's essay was written for, "and prefixed to," the Supplement to the fourth, fifth, and sixth editions of the *Encyclopædia Britannica*.

25. Miller, *Retrospect*, II, 11–12.

26. Thomas Reid, *Essays on the Powers of the Human Mind* (Edinburgh, 1812), II, 138–39.

27. Although Reid had a lasting and pervasive influence on Common Sense thought, later Scottish realists never regarded his metaphysical position as incontestable orthodoxy. See for example, Sir William Hamilton's edition of *The Works of Thomas Reid, D. D.*, 2 vols. (Edinburgh, 1853), II, 812–13, where Hamilton comments that at times Reid's ideas are "perhaps imperfectly developed, rather than deliberately wrong." The best study of the wide implications of Scottish thought is Gladys Bryson, *Man and Society: The Scottish Inquiry of the Eighteenth Century* (Princeton, 1945). See also Torgny Torgnysson Segerstedt, *The Problem of Knowledge in Scottish Philosophy* (Lund, 1935) and Meredydd Evans, "Perception and Common Sense in the Writings of Thomas Reid" (Ph. D. dissertation, Princeton, 1955, Microfilm Publication No. 13,690). S. A. Grave's *The Scottish Philosophy of Common Sense* (Oxford, 1960), which unfortunately came to my hand too late for me to make use of in this study, is now the most thorough and systematic analysis of the origins and nature of Common Sense thought.

28. *The Philosophy of Reid*, ed. with an introduction by E. Hershey Sneath (New York, 1892), p. 50.

29. Friedrich Ueberweg, *History of Philosophy* (New York, 1884), II, 415, Appendix I: "Philosophy in Great Britain and America."

30. See Benjamin Rand, "Philosophical Instruction in Harvard University from 1636 to 1900," *Harvard Graduates Magazine*, XXXVII (1928–29), 196–97.

31. Hamilton, *Works of Reid*, II, 805.

32. Ibid., p. 810.

33. Ibid., p. 811.

34. Ibid., p. 812.

35. *The Works of Dugald Stewart*, 7 vols. (Cambridge, [Mass.], 1829), I, 355.

36. Ibid., III, 214.

37. Ibid., p. 212.

38. Ibid., I, 381–82.

39. Ibid., p. 385.

40. Ibid., pp. 388–90.

41. Beattie, *Dissertations*, I, 87–89.

42. Ibid., II, 320. For a view of the Scottish attitude toward fiction (and by extension the American attitude as well) in the larger con-

text of a neoclassical suspicion of the imagination, see W. F. Gallaway, "The Conservative Attitude toward Fiction, 1770–1830," *PMLA*, LV (1946), 1041–59. Among others, Gallaway cites Beattie and Stewart. "The neo-classical hostility to the imagination," he writes, "and the contrasting respect for judgment and reality form the background for the widespread objection to fiction which developed false ideas of life and rendered the reader (generally the adolescent is meant) unfit for the monotony of everyday life" (p. 1052). See also two articles by Donald F. Bond, "Distrust of the Imagination in English Neo-Classicism," *Philological Quarterly*, XIV (1935), 54–69, and "The Neo-Classical Psychology of the Imagination," *ELH*, IV (1937), 245–64.

43. Thomas Brown, *Lectures on the Philosophy of the Human Mind* (Edinburgh, 1845), pp. 451–52.

44. Henry Home Kames, *Elements of Criticism* (Edinburgh, 1762), I, 7.

45. Ibid., p. 13.

Chapter Three

1. Levi Frisbie, *Inaugural Address, Delivered in the Chapel of the University at Cambridge, November 5, 1817* (Cambridge, [Mass.], 1817), p. 22.

2. James Beattie, *Dissertations Moral and Critical*, 2 vols. (Dublin, 1783), I, 9.

3. Ibid., pp. 89–90.

4. See Martin Kallich, "The Association of Ideas and Critical Theory: Hobbes, Locke, and Addison," *ELH*, XII (1945), 290–315. Gordon McKenzie has pointed out Kames's place in the mechanist tradition: "Lord Kames and the Mechanist Tradition," in *Essays and Studies*, University of California Studies in English, No. 14 (1943), pp. 93–121. For a larger consideration of associationism and mechanism, see Martin Kallich, "The Associationist Criticism of Francis Hutcheson and David Hume," *Studies in Philology*, XLIII (1946), 644–67, and "The Association of Ideas and Akenside's *Pleasures of Imagination*," *Modern Language Notes*, LXII (1947), 166–73; and Gordon McKenzie, *Critical Responsiveness: A Study of the Psychological Current in Later Eighteenth-Century Criticism*,

University of California Studies in English, No. 20 (1949), especially
Chapter VI, "Imagination," pp. 180–206.

5. *Biographia Literaria*, ed. J. Shawcross, 2 vols. (Oxford, 1907),
I, 202. Newton P. Stallknecht studies Coleridge's imagination in the
Biographia Literaria in *Strange Seas of Thought* (Durham, N. C.,
1945), pp. 258–67.

6. In his study, *Coleridge as Philosopher* (London and New
York, 1930), John H. Muirhead points out (pp. 198–99) Coleridge's need for both a new psychology and a new metaphysics:
"In view of the defects of current theories, what he felt to be required was first a psychology that would explain the working of
imagination as not merely a reproductive, but a creative process;
and, secondly, a metaphysic that would account for the appeal
which its creations make to what is deepest in the soul of man."
From my own point of view, however, it seems that Coleridge's
new psychology presupposes a new metaphysics.

7. M. H. Abrams, *The Mirror and the Lamp: Romantic Theory
and the Critical Tradition* (New York, The Norton Library, 1958),
p. 283.

8. James Mackintosh, "Ethical Philosophy—Eighteenth Century," in *Dissertations on the History of Metaphysical and Ethical
. . . Science* (Edinburgh, 1835), pp. 387–88.

9. *The Works of Thomas Reid, D. D.*, ed. Sir William Hamilton, 2 vols. (Edinburgh, 1863), I, 421. For an account of Reid's
philosophical position as set forth in the *Essays on the Intellectual
Powers of Man*, see A. D. Woozley's introduction to his edition of
the *Essays* (London, 1941), pp. vii–xl.

10. *Works of Reid*, ibid., pp. 422, 425.

11. *Elements of Criticism*, ed. James R. Boyd (New York, 1868),
p. 63. See the chapter on Kames in Walter John Hipple, Jr., *The
Beautiful, The Sublime, and the Picturesque in Eighteenth-Century
British Aesthetic Theory* (Carbondale [Illinois], 1957), pp. 99–121.
Mr. Hipple also includes chapter-length considerations of Hume,
Blair, Reid, Alison, and Stewart. He considers, quite correctly it
seems to me in the light of what the Scots were doing, that "the
common sense and intuitive senses of the Scottish school are quite
consistent with empiricism" (p. 341, n.).

12. *Collected Papers of Charles Sanders Peirce*, ed. Charles Hart-
shorne and Paul Weiss, 6 vols. (Cambridge, [Mass.], 1931–35), V,

354. For a description of the differences between Peirce's Critical Common-Sensism and Scottish Common Sense thought, see Chapter IV.

13. *Aids to Reflection* (Burlington, Vt., 1829), pp. lii, 1.

14. Ibid., pp. xliv–xlv. Harry Hayden Clark writes: "The manner in which the transcendentalists centered their massed arguments against mechanism is ample proof of how pervasive and weighty an obstacle to their own ends the concept of mechanism actually was, especially as constituting the semi-official concept taught in our universities by spokesmen of the Scottish 'Common Sense' philosophy"—in "Changing Attitudes in Early American Literary Criticism: 1800–1840," *The Development of American Literary Criticism*, ed. Floyd Stovall (Chapel Hill, N. C., 1955), p. 68.

15. Lewis S. Feuer, "James Marsh and the Conservative Transcendentalist Philosophy: A Political Interpretation," *New England Quarterly*, XXI (1958), 21.

16. In his *Three Christian Transcendentalists: James Marsh, Caleb Sprague Henry, and Frederic Henry Hedge* (New York, 1943), Ronald V. Wells comments (p. 2) that in philosophy "all three had made their way through Locke and the Scottish intuitionists." Most of the transcendentalists, Wells says later (p. 11), received their training in New England colleges, "where in the first third of the nineteenth century Locke was either supplanted or supplemented by the writings of Reid, Hamilton, and Stewart." Wells's term "Scottish intuitionists" exemplifies the kind of terminology the Scots have called upon themselves. For some they are realists, for others intuitionists. Whenever they are seen contributing to the making of a transcendentalist, one may expect to find the intuitionist label: they differed from Locke; they relied on intuition; therefore, they are intuitionists. If one keeps the whole of the Common Sense inquiry in mind, however, and understands what budding transcendentalist thinkers could do with key Scottish terms, he finds, as I have attempted to show, that the Scots relied on instinct and intuition only as means to construct a valid philosophical realism. First and foremost, the Scots were realists; their special problem was to keep their means (ambiguous, perhaps even anomalous) from subverting their ends.

17. *The Works of Orestes A. Brownson*, 20 vols. (Detroit, 1882–87), I, 101.

18. Ibid., p. 95. The quotation and the following discussion come from the section on "Imagination" in Brownson's essay "Synthetic Philosophy," first published in the *Democratic Review,* 1842–43.

19. Ibid., pp. 95–96.

20. Ibid., p. 99.

21. Ibid., pp. 101–2.

22. Ibid., p. 105.

23. Ibid., p. 106. Any one who supposes that "the Ideal is the mere creation of the subject," says Brownson, makes the "essence of poetry consist in *fiction.* Fiction is that which is *made up* by the poet out of himself, his own fancies and conceits, and needs, and has no objective basis. All the truth or reality there is in poetry, and therefore in imagination, on this hypothesis, is simply and exclusively of the subject's own creating. But this is by no means true" (I, 100). Since, for Brownson, every object of imagination is a not-me with independent ideal existence, it follows that there can be no such thing a pure fiction; in his terms, such being is impossible.

24. *The Works of Dugald Stewart,* 7 vols. (Cambridge [Mass.], 1829), IV, 368–71. Stewart's analysis is entitled "On the Culture of certain intellectual Habits connected with the first Elements of Taste"; it is the fourth of his *Philosophical Essays, Works,* IV, 368–91.

25. Ibid., I, 381–84.

26. Ibid., p. 382.

27. Ibid., p. 379.

28. Ibid., p. 388.

29. Ibid., p. 385.

30. Ibid., pp. 389–90.

31. See R. W. G. Vail, "Susanna Haswell Rowson, the Author of *Charlotte Temple:* A Bibliographical Study," *Proceedings of the American Antiquarian Society,* n.s., LXII (1932), pt. 1, 47–160. The last edition of *Charlotte Temple* was edited with a lengthy introduction by Francis W. Halsey, 2 vols. in 1 (New York, 1905). In his *Mathew Carey: Editor, Author and Publisher* (New York, 1921), Earl L. Bradsher suggests that the great vogue of *Charlotte Temple* was in part due to "persistent advertising" (p. 25); Carey's firm published nine editions of the novel. Bradsher cites a letter of 1812 from Carey to Mrs. Rowson which claims that "the sales of Charlotte Temple exceed those of any of the most celebrated novels

that ever appeared in England" (p. 50). Perhaps the most amusing evidence of the popularity of *Charlotte* exists in the letters of the energetic bookseller Parson Weems to Matthew Carey entreating or demanding copies of the novel for his customers: see *Mason Locke Weems, His Works and Ways,* ed. Emily Ellsworth Ford Skeel, 3 vols. (New York, 1929).

32. Mrs. Rowson twice departed from this self-imposed renunciation of fiction. The first of these occasions was during the period from 1802 to 1805 while she edited the *Boston Weekly Magazine,* when her story "Sincerity" appeared in that periodical in thirty-three installments. It was later collected and published by Charles Williams of Boston as *Sarah; or, The Exemplary Wife.* The second instance consisted of her writing *Charlotte's Daughter; or, the Three Orphans. A Sequel to Charlotte Temple,* which was not published, however, until 1828, after her death. Mrs. Rowson did continue to write poetry and essays after the foundation of her school for girls, a fact which implies a distinction in her mind between the novel and other literary forms. In 1804 she published her *Miscellaneous Poems* by subscription. In later years her poetry grew devotional, and she became increasingly occupied with writing textbooks for her school.

33. Henry Sherburne, *Oriental Philanthropist; or, True Republican* (Portsmouth, N. H., 1800), pp. 3–8.

34. Samuel Woodworth, *The Champions of Freedom; or, The Mysterious Chief* (New York, 1816), I, iii–viii. Woodworth has been most popularly known as the author of "The Old Oaken Bucket," though in the 1820's and 1830's he achieved some popularity as a dramatist. His *The Forest Rose; or, American Farmers* (1825) "was one of the longest-lived American plays before the Civil War" (see Oral Sumner Coad, "The Plays of Samuel Woodworth," *Sewanee Review,* XXVII [1919], 166.)

35. Such a subtitle and the tone of much of the preface and the story may be Brown's way of reacting to the manner in which the bizarre though hyperserious *The Power of Sympathy* (1789)—"Founded in Truth"—was (or was not) received. To illustrate the tragic effects of seduction in *The Power of Sympathy,* Brown had made use of an actual case history, that of Frances Theodora Apthorp, which had caused much indignation in Boston not five months before. In his *Specimens of Newspaper Literature,* 2 vols. (Boston, 1850), Joseph T. Buckingham says that an attempt was

made to suppress the novel immediately upon its publication (I, 323). Milton Ellis disagrees, however, pointing out the little attention given to the novel by Boston newspapers, and blames Buckingham for creating the idea that the novel became a sensation and was "denounced in the press and the pulpit" ("The Author of the First American Novel," *American Literature*, IV [1933], 366). Tremaine McDowell prints copies of letters which "purport" to be "the last recorded words of Frances Theodora Apthorp, sister of Mrs. Sara Apthorp Morton," together with a concise summary of the situation, in "Last Words of a Sentimental Heroine," *American Literature*, IV (1932), 174–77. Mrs. Sarah Apthorp (Wentworth) Morton, the early American poet, was long regarded as the author of *The Power of Sympathy*, undoubtedly because of her family connection with the principals in the scandal. Whatever happened in Boston because of the novel, William Hill Brown must have found cause in it to react with *Ira and Isabella*, which, however, he did not publish before his death in 1793.

36. William Hill Brown, *Ira and Isabella; or, the Natural Children. A Novel, Founded in Fiction*. . . (Boston, 1807), pp. iv–v. Marmontel's "Moral Tales" appeared in translation in *The Novelist's Magazine*, Vol. IV, 1783 (along with "Peregrine Pickle"), which would have been available to Brown. He drew his observations specifically from Marmontel's "Original Preface" and from the opening paragraph of "The Four Phials" (p. 33). The name "Xixzoffou" might be a corruption, deliberate or not, of Xisuthros, the Greek transcription of the Sumerian name Ziusudra. Xisuthros corresponds to the Biblical Noah: he was advised by the gods to save himself and his family from the flood by building a ship. There is the strong probability, however, that Brown has simply invented the name.

37. Ibid., pp. x–xi.

38. One of the most interesting, albeit adventitious, features of *Ira and Isabella* is the "Scale of Novelists" with which Brown ends his preface. He gives no principle of selection, no reason, for example, why Fielding and Goldsmith are omitted, and no information as to his scale of grading, which may well be on the basis of twenty, with no one absolutely perfect. He simply wonders how the different romance and novel writers of Europe have excelled in the various aspects of their work; for the sake of brevity, he condenses his thoughts on the subject into the following "SCALE OF NOVELISTS":

Author	Genius	Satire	Knowledge	TASTE			
				Intellig.	Imagin.	Style	Pathos
Cervantes	19	19	17	16	18	15	13
Rabelais	15	18	17	15	13	10	7
Le Sage	14	17	12	12	14	11	6
Rousseau	16	10	13	15	15	17	16
Fénelon	16	7	15	16	14	17	14
Marmontel	14	10	11	15	15	17	16
Smollet	11	16	10	9	14	6	5
Richardson	19	11	12	16	17	17	18
Swift	18	19	17	18	18	17	14
De Foe	11	4	10	10	15	6	10
Sterne	18	15	14	14	16	17	19
Miss Burney	14	11	12	16	16	16	17
Miss Smith	13	9	12	15	15	14	9
Johnson	18	15	19	18	18	19	15
Gesner	10	6	11	15	15	16	16
Mad. Genlis	12	10	10	12	13	15	12
Dr. Dodd	11	9	12	10	13	10	13
Voltaire	18	17	18	16	18	16	13

Judged in this fashion, the five most significant writers would be Johnson 122, Swift 121, Cervantes 117, Voltaire 116, and Richardson 110.

39. Perry Miller remarks that Edwards' originality was "not substantive but primarily verbal—which justifies calling him an artist—although his innovation in language portended an ultimate revolution in substance" (*Jonathan Edwards* [New York, 1949], p. 48). For an analysis showing the literary quality of an Edwards sermon, see Edwin H. Cady, "The Artistry of Jonathan Edwards," *New England Quarterly*, XXII (1949), 61–72.

40. Benjamin T. Spencer brilliantly examines the complexities of the attempt to express a national identity in *The Quest for Nationality* (Syracuse, 1957).

41. In the hands of Richardson, of course, the sentimental novel, avowedly didactic in purpose, had achieved a peculiar power of its own. But not only did Richardson have a degree of talent far superior to that of any of these early American sentimental novelists; he could employ that talent to explore and re-explore the significance of broadly domestic tensions in terms of an always implicit social framework. Richardson *assumes* society even in the

most apparently private letters of his novels; and the quality of his assumption helps to sustain his minute fictional analysis. The elements of didacticism and domesticity in his work could and did serve the needs of the American novelist, but the prevailing social implications of Richardson's world, which gave meaning to novelistic incident, could not be duplicated. The American novelist, in effect, took what he wanted and needed; but even here he was deceived. For what he most wanted and needed were forms, and what he took were conventions—abstracted and cut off from that which gave them formal significance—which he had to make do, or try to make do, as forms.

42. The task of the writer of fiction was at least distinct from, if not more difficult than, that of the writer of poetry. The relative newness of the novel form deprived the novelist of the opportunity to invoke traditionally great works of the same genre as an allusive way to safety. But the poet too had his problems. The early American poet William C. Foster complains of the neglect of poets and poetry in the preface to his *Poetry on Different Subjects* (1805). He states that he is offering his work to the public "with diffidence," at a time "when Poetry is scarcely read, and the Poet scarce receives a smile, even among the friends of literature." Although one may truly say that "poetry is in its fallen state, . . . what is the cause of its decline? Is it because the fire of genius which animated a Virgil glows not in the bosom of the modern poet, or that a sufficient encouragement is not offered for its progression? It must be attributed to the latter; for he who would, at the present day, strive to live by literary pursuits, must starve in the attempt! And the poet may think himself handsomely recompensed if any at this *enlightened age* will condescend to read his poems. O, Poesy! what but the friendship of the Muses, and the pleasures of fancy, are the rewards of the bard?" (pp. vii, xi). This is no apology for poetry as imaginatively rendered experience, but the ageless economic lament of the artist, which any of the early novelists could have duplicated had there not been more important things for them to discuss. For analyses of poetic attitudes and achievement in the United States, see Roy Harvey Pearce, "On the Continuity of American Poetry," *Hudson Review*, X (1957–58), 518–39, and Donald M. Foerster, "Homer, Milton, and the American Revolt Against Epic Poetry: 1812–1860," *Studies in Philology*, LIII (1956), 75–100.

43. *The Portable Melville*, ed. Jay Leyda (New York, 1952),

from a letter to E. A. Duyckinck, p. 379; George Santayana, *Interpretations of Poetry and Religion* (New York: Harper Torchbook, 1957), p. 219. J. T. Flanagan studies "Emerson as a Critic of Fiction," *Philological Quarterly*, XV (1936), 36–45.

44. See Marion L. Kesselring, *Hawthorne's Reading, 1828–1850* (New York, 1949).

45. Beattie, *Dissertations*, I, 113.

Chapter Four

1. Roy Harvey Pearce, "Hawthorne and the Twilight of Romance," *Yale Review*, XXXVII (1948), 504. See also Jesse Bier, "Hawthorne on the Romance: His Prefaces Related and Examined," *Modern Philology*, LIII (1955), pp. 17–24.

2. Charles Feidelson, Jr., *Symbolism and American Literature* (Chicago, 1953), p. 43.

3. Harry Levin, *The Power of Blackness: Hawthorne, Poe, Melville* (New York, 1958), pp. 18, 240.

4. Richard Chase, *The American Novel and Its Tradition* (New York: Anchor Books, 1957), p. viii.

5. Walter E. Houghton, *The Victorian Frame of Mind: 1830–1870* (New Haven, 1957), p. 110.

6. See Donald F. Bond's "Distrust of the Imagination in English Neo-Classicism," *Philological Quarterly*, XIV (1935), 54–69 and "The Neo-Classical Psychology of the Imagination," *ELH*, IV (1937), 245–64. Also W. F. Gallaway, "The Conservative Attitude toward Fiction, 1770–1830," *PMLA*, LV (1946), 1041–59.

7. Richard D. Altick, *The English Common Reader* (Chicago, 1957), p. 64.

8. Ian Watt, *The Rise of the Novel* (London, 1957), p. 39. Mr. Watt discusses social and economic factors pertaining to the growth of the reading class in the eighteenth century, pp. 35–39.

9. Houghton, *Victorian Frame of Mind*, p. 117.

10. Changing styles of the horrific are amusingly pointed out in a recent "Freddie" comic strip, in which six-year-old Freddie is talking to four-year-old Ernest: Panel 1, "Yep, Ernest, ol' time people worried about some mighty foolish stuff." Panel 2, "Goblins! Dragons! Werewolfs! Ha!!" Panel 3, "This is a bran' new age!!" Panel 4 (with Freddie and Ernest looking fearfully skyward), "All

WE gotta worry about is horrible monsters from outer space!!"
The imagination seems always able to find material for fright.

11. *The Writings of Thomas Jefferson,* ed. Albert Ellery Bergh
(Washington, D. C., 1907), XV, 166, letter to Nathaniel Burwell,
March 14, 1818. Jefferson admitted that some works among this
"mass of trash" were relatively unobjectionable because founded on
real life and the principles of morality. Marmontel's new moral tales
("but not his old ones, which are really immoral") and the "writings of Miss Edgeworth" are among this group.

12. Elizabeth Sewell, "The Death of the Imagination," *Thought,*
XXVIII (1953), 439. For an analysis of the modes and meanings of
contemporary science fiction, see Robert Plank, "Lighter Than
Air, but Heavy as Hate," *Partisan Review,* XXIV (1957), 106–16.
See also Stephen O. Mitchell, "Alien Vision: The Techniques of
Science Fiction," *Modern Fiction Studies,* IV (1958–59), 346–56.

13. W. H. Auden, "Balaam and the Ass: The Master-Servant
Relation in Literature," *Thought,* XXIX (1954), 260.

14. Elizabeth Sewell, "Death of Imagination," p. 432.

15. James McCosh, *Realistic Philosophy,* 2 vols. (New York,
1890), I, 3.

16. James McCosh, *Philosophy of Reality: Should It Be Favored
By America?* (New York, 1894), p. 66.

17. G. Stanley Hall, "Philosophy in the United States," *Mind,*
IV (1879), 90.

18. Ibid., p. 99.

19. Ibid., pp. 103–4.

20. *Collected Papers of Charles Sanders Peirce,* ed. Charles Hart-
shorne and Paul Weiss, 6 vols. (Cambridge [Mass.], 1931–35), I,
353. Peirce writes earlier: "A man may say 'I will content myself
with common sense.' I, for one, am with him there, in the main. I
shall show why I do not think there can be any *direct* profit in
going behind common sense—meaning by common sense those ideas
and beliefs that man's situation absolutely forces upon him" (I, 52).

21. Ibid., V, 355–66.

22. Ibid., p. 297.

23. Ibid., I, 20–21.

24. Ibid., p. 52.

INDEX

Abrahms, M. H., 111
Addison, Joseph, 39, 43
Ahlstrom, Sydney E., 19, 20
Akenside, Dr. Mark, 123
Alexander, Archibald, 20
Alford Professorship at Harvard, 17, 47, 147
Alison, Archibald, 32, 39, 49, 110, 145
Alonzo and Melissa, 144
Altick, Richard D., 154
Amelia, or The Faithless Briton, 80
American Quarterly Review, 14
American Philosophical Society, 13
American Review, The, 43
American Review of History and Politics, 38
Amherst College, 24
Andover Theological Seminary, 20, 22, 35
Associate Reformed Church, 64
Association psychology, 32, 39, 110
Astor, John Jacob, 43
Auden, W. H., 159–61, 164
Augusta College, 21

Bancroft, George, 39
Barlow, Joel, 19
Beasley, The Rev. Frederick, 5
Beattie, James: influence on S. S. Smith, 14; at Yale, 19; used to improve Kames, 25; general influence, 26, 32, 116; criticism of, 31, 43; sees fiction opposed to history, 73, 101; on imagination, 101–2,

Beattie, James (cont.)
108–9, 110; warns against fiction, 101–2; on night terrors, 145, 146–47; mentioned, 35, 118
Bentham, Jeremy, 155
Berkeley, George, 3, 4, 5, 14, 27–28, 30, 33, 42, 85, 91, 94, 163
Bishop, Robert Hamilton, 21
Blackwell, Thomas, 71
Blair, Hugh, 15, 19, 24, 25, 26, 32, 33, 53, 71, 132
Bleecker, Ann Eliza, 82
Boarding School, The, 82
Boston Magazine, 24
Bowdoin College, 25
Bowen, Francis, 15, 17, 33, 34, 88, 176
Boyd, The Rev. James R., 25
Brackenridge, Hugh Henry, 6
Brinton, Crane, 73
Bristed, C. A., 40, 43-45, 54, 115
Brown, Charles Brockden, 24, 148
Brown, Herbert Ross, 57, 59
Brown, Thomas: importance to Levi Hedge, 15–16, to Emerson, 33, to Brownson, 34–35, to Samuel Gilman, 38-39; at Yale, 19; general influence, 25, 116; supersedes Locke as text, 30–31; criticism of, 31, 41–42, 44; controversial ideas of, 35–36; on fiction, 102; read by Hawthorne, 145; mentioned, 3, 18, 49, 53
Brown, William Hill, 82, 131–35, 156

193

Brown University, 24, 25
Brownson, Orestes, 34–36, 117–21, 122, 140
Brunck, Richard François Phillipe, 18
Bryant, William Cullen, 32, 39, 53
Burr, Aaron, 6
Burton, The Rev. Asa, 25
Butler, Bishop Joseph, 47

Calvinistic tradition, American, 19
Cambridge University, 43
Campbell, Thomas, 31, 44, 115
Canonsburg Academy (Jefferson College), 20, 24
Caritat, Hocquet, 29
Carlyle, Thomas, 44, 115, 155
Cervantes, Miguel de, 58
Champions of Freedom, The, 128–31
Channing, Edward T., 15, 33, 39
Channing, Walter, 39
Charlotte Temple, 80, 127
Charvat, William, 15, 24, 37–38, 113
Chase, Richard, 152–53
Chinard, Gilbert, 7, 8
Christian Examiner, 39
Christian Spectator, 19
Clap, Thomas, 18
Coleridge, Samuel T., 23, 44, 110–11, 112, 115, 116, 122, 127
Columbia University, 24
Congregationalists, 21
Congreve, William, 141
Constantius and Pulchera, 144
Contrast, The, 155–56
Cooper, James Fenimore, 50, 57, 130
Cooper, Thomas, 30, 31–32, 139
Coquette, The, 80, 82, 126
Cousin, Victor, 23
Cudworth, Ralph, 36, 47
Curti, Merle, 4, 17

Dartmouth College, 23
Darwin, Charles, 162
Davis, Merrell, 32
Dennie, Joseph, 15, 76–79, 8⁴
Descartes, René, 121
Dickinson, John, 9

Dickinson College, 22
Durbin, The Rev. John P., 21–22
Dwight, Timothy, 19

Edgeworth, Maria, 57, 58
Edinburgh Review, 32, 38
Edwards, Jonathan, 136, 137
Ely, Ezra Stiles, 26–27
Emerson, Ralph Waldo, 32–33, 53, 54, 107, 117, 121, 122, 133, 140, 162
Emerson, William, 33
Emerson, The Rev. William, 175–76
Emily Hamilton, 81–82, 126
Everett, Alexander H., 40–43, 44, 45, 112

Farmer's Library, 32
Feidelson, Charles, Jr., 152
Female Quixotism, 126, 156
Ferguson, Adam, 9, 14
Feuer, Lewis S., 116
Fiction: mistrust of, 46, 57; and metaphysics, 73, 75, 76, 78, 79, 82, 84. See also Gray, The Rev. Dr. James; Common Sense and, 88, 97–101, 101–2; history antidote for, 73–74; creation of, 126; didactic, 126–27, 135, 138; pseudo-didactic, 127–28, 135, 138; "sports," 128–35 passim, 138; history opposed to, 73, 101, 130–31, 133; the romance, 141–45, 151–53; and "disengaged" experience, 143–44; and "haunted mind," 148; Jefferson on, 158; Elizabeth Sewell on, 159; English suspicion of, 153–54; English and American attitudes compared, 154–55
Foster, Hannah Webster, 82, 126
Franklin, Benjamin, 10–11, 53, 169
Freneau, Philip, 6
Frisbie, Levi, 15, 17, 33, 37, 40, 45–50, 52, 107, 139
Froude, James Anthony, 155
Fuller, Margaret, 50

Gamesters, The, 126
Gardiner, W. H., 39
Geneva College, 24
Gentz, Frederick, 12

Gerando, Marie Joseph de, 18
Giles, Joel, 33
Gilman, Samuel, 18, 38–39, 44, 53
Godwin, William, 47
Grave, S. A., 182
Gray, The Rev. Dr. James, 64–74, 75, 76, 78, 79, 97, 100–101, 107, 158, 164
Green, Ashbel, 13

Hall, G. Stanley, 3, 11, 162–63
Hamilton, Alexander, 136
Hamilton, Sir William, 3, 36, 85, 88–94, 96, 114, 162
Hamilton College, 24
Hampden-Sydney College, 13, 22
Hapless Orphan, The, 80
Harris, William T., 163
Harvard University, 15–18, 20, 32–34, 40
"Haunted Mind, The," 145–48
Hawthorne, Nathaniel, 50, 140, 141, 144, 145–48, 151, 152, 153, 163
Hazlitt, William, 44, 115
Hedge, Levi, 15–17, 19, 33
Hegel, Georg Wilhelm Friedrich, 162, 163
History of Maria Kittle, The, 82
Hobbes, Thomas, 39, 47, 110
Hodge, Charles, 20
Houghton, Walter E., 153, 155
Howard, Leon, 18, 34
Hudnutt, William H., III, 13
Hudson, W. P., 32
Hume, David, 3, 4, 14, 26, 27–28, 30, 33, 35, 39, 42, 85, 91, 94, 163
Hutcheson, Francis, 39
Huxley, Thomas Henry, 163

Imagination: mistrust of, 57, 61, 95–97, 101–2, 107–8, 130, 138, 148; danger of fiction for, 67, 72, 77, 81–82, 83, 97–101; and order of possibility, 70–71, 90, 91, 94, 95–96; and anti-primitivism, 71–72; value of history for, 73–74; beings of imagination, 94; control of by Common Sense, 108, 146–47; Common Sense idea of, 108–12; mech-

Imagination (cont.)
anism, 109–10, 130, 144; Coleridge on, 110–11; Brownson on, 117–21; Stewart on cultivation of, 122–25; transcendental imagination, 139–40; and "disengaged" experience, 144; and "haunted mind," 147–48; Elizabeth Sewell on, 158–61; W. H. Auden on, 159–61; Jefferson on, 160–61; English suspicion of, 153–54; difference between English and American suspicion of, 154–57
Indiana University, 21
Innatism, 41, 42, 112, 114
Ira and Isabella, 131–35, 156

James, Henry, 50, 117, 133, 142–44
Jarvis, Samuel F., 61–63, 74, 76, 78, 79
Jefferson, Thomas, 7–9, 11, 53, 136, 137, 158, 160–61
Jones, The Rev. William, 62–63
Julia and the Illuminated Baron, 80, 144

Kallich, Martin, 39, 110
Kames, Lord: Jefferson's view of, 7–8; influence of Locke on, 7; friend of Franklin's, 10–11, 169; criticism of, 13–14, 43–44; influence on E. T. Channing, 15; educational influence, 19, 22, 23–24; general influence, 25, 26, 32, 116; mentioned, 35, 49, 53, 115, 123
Kant, Immanuel, 23, 40, 162, 163, 164
Kingsley, Charles, 155
Knapp, John, 39
Koch, Adrienne, 7, 11
Kwiat, Joseph, 33

Ladd, Joesph, 24
Last Resource, The, or Female Fortitude, 80
Lee, Charles, 6
Lee, Henry, 6
Levin, Harry, 152
Lindly, The Rev. Jacob, 21
Linn, John Blair, 24

Locke, John: influence on Kames, 7, on Brownson, 34, on A. H. Everett, 40–41, 42, 43; S. S. Smith on, 14; James Bowen on, 17; educational influence, 17–18, 19, 25, 30; his epistemology, 17–18, 43; criticism of, 18, 30; general influence, 25, 26, 29, 32, 116, 139; mentioned, 4, 39, 43, 68, 85, 91, 114
Lowell, James Russell, 34, 53, 121
Lucinda; or, the Mountain Mourner, 80–81
Lynch, William F., S. J., 180

Macauley, Thomas Babington, 155
McCosh, James, 162, 167
Mackintosh, James, 112
McMillan, The Rev. John, 21
Madison, James, 6, 136
Mahan, Asa, 22-23
Manning, Mary, 145
Manvill, Mrs. P. D., 80–81
Marsh, James, 30, 54, 116–17, 139, 140
Melville, Herman, 140, 148
Methodists, 21–22
Miami University, 21
Middlebury College, 23, 24
Mill, John Stuart, 163
Miller, Perry, 138
Miller, Samuel, 5, 13, 27–29, 74–76, 78, 79, 86, 107
Monima; or, The Beggar Girl, 80
Monthly Anthology and Boston Review, 29–30
Moral philosophy course, 18, 23–24

Nisbet, The Rev. Charles, 22, 23
Norris, Frank, 153
North American Review, 15, 16, 18, 38, 39, 40, 45
North Carolina University, 24
Nott, Eliphalet, 22, 23

Oberlin College, 22–23
Ohio University, 21
Orians, G. Harrison, 57, 59
Oriental Philanthropist, 128
Oswald, James, 31

Paley, William, 19, 32
Palmer, Ormond E., 57, 59
Papashvily, Helen W., 127
Park, Edwards Amasa, 20, 172
Pearce, Roy Harvey, 4, 7, 151
Peirce, C. S., 114, 163–64, 165
Pennsylvania, Univ. of, 5, 9, 24
Philadelphia Academy for the Instruction of Young Ladies, 64
Philadelphia Bible Society, 64
Plato, 121, 128, 140
Poe, Edgar Allan, 148
Port Folio, The, 76
Porter, Noah, 88
Power of Sympathy, The, 79, 82, 131, 134
Presbyterians, 4, 20–23
Prescott, W. H., 37, 53
Princeton Theological Seminary, 20
Princeton University, 5, 6, 13, 20–22, 53
Progress of Romance, The, 58

Raeburn, Sir Henry, 38
Rahv, Philip, 134
Rand, Benjamin, 14, 18
Read, Mrs. Martha, 80, 81
Reeve, Clara, 58, 141
Reid, Thomas: influence on James Wilson, 9–10, 11; praised by S. S. Smith, 14, by Samuel Miller, 28–29, by C. S. Peirce, 164; general influence, 25–27, 64, 108, 116; criticism of, 30, 31, 41, 42, 43; influence on Emerson, 33, on Thoreau, 33, on Brownson, 34, 36; metaphysical principles, 86–88, 94, 109; on instinct and common sense, 112–15; mentioned, 3, 5, 16, 35, 37, 38, 49, 53, 85, 89, 91, 93, 117, 162
Riley, I. Woodbridge, 4, 11, 54
Rossiter, Clinton, 12
Rousseau, Jean Jacques, 47
Rowson, Susanna, 126–27, 135, 138
Rush, Benjamin, 6, 9

Santayana, George, 140
Schmidt, George P., 21, 23

Schmucker, Samuel S., 36
Schneider, Herbert W., 4
Scott, John Robert, 71
Scott, Sir Walter, 57, 130
Seward, Frederick W., 22
Sewell, Elizabeth, 158–61
Sherburne, Henry, 128–32
Simms, William Gilmore, 151
Smiles, Samuel, 155, 156
Smith, Adam, 9
Smith, Charles Page, 9
Smith, John Blair, 22, 23
Smith, Samuel Stanhope, 13–14, 22
Smith, Wilson, 173
Socrates, 121
Sparks, Jared, 39
Spencer, Benjamin T., 24
Spencer, Herbert, 163
Stewart, Dugald: Jefferson's respect
    for, 8, 11; influence on S. S.
    Smith, 14, on Emerson, 32–33, on
    Thoreau, 33, on James Russell
    Lowell, 34, on Brownson, 34;
    praised by Samuel Gilman, 18, by
    Hocquet Caritat, 29, by *Monthly
    Anthology*. . . , 29–30, by Robert
    Walsh, 38, by A. H. Everett, 41,
    by Levi Frisbie, 47; educational
    influence, 16, 18, 19, 23, 24, 30–31;
    general influence, 25–27, 32, 108,
    116; criticism of, 26–27, 31, 43; his
    anti-primitivism, 71, 123–25; on
    dangers of fiction and imagina-
    tion, 95–101; allies mechanism and
    Common Sense, 109–10; on the
    cultivated imagination, 122–25;
    read by Hawthorne, 145; men-
    tioned, 3, 16, 35, 36, 38, 49, 53, 85,
    93, 109, 130, 162
Stewart, Mrs. Dugald, 177
Stockton, Richard, 6
Streeter, Robert E., 39

Tappan, David, 15, 20
Taylor, Nathaniel William, 20
Tenney, Tabitha, 126

Thayer, Caroline Matilda Warren,
    126
Thoreau, Henry David, 33, 34, 53,
    54, 117, 121, 140
Tocqueville, Alexis de, 12
Todd, Edgeley W., 14, 18
Tracy, Destutt de, 8
Transylvania College, 24
Trumbull, John, 19
Tudor, William, 39
Twain, Mark, 144
Tyler, Royall, 155

Union College, 22, 24
Upham, Thomas C., 25, 36, 162

Vermont, University of, 30
Verplanck, C. G., 39
Vickery, Sukey, 81–82, 126
Vincennes University, 21

Walker, James, 15, 17
Walsh, Robert, 38, 53
Warren, Mercy, 17
Washington, George, 9
Washington, Martha, 9
Washington College, 24
Watson, The Rev. John, 21
Watt, Ian, 154
Wayland, Francis, 23, 25–26, 32, 162
Wesleyan University, 24
Wheaton, Henry, 48
Whitman, Elizabeth, 82–84
Whitman, Walt, 121, 140–41
Willard, Sidney, 15
Williams College, 24
Wilson, James, 7, 9–10, 11, 53
Witherspoon, John, 5, 6, 13, 22
Wollaston, William, 18, 19
Woods, Leonard, 20
Woodworth, Samuel, 128–31, 132
Wright, Louis B., 21

Yale Divinity School, 20
Yale University, 18–19, 21, 35, 43
Youman, E. L., 163

Date Due

	PRINTED	IN U. S. A.	